Copyright © 2012 by Green Olive Books

All rights reserved.

Permission is granted to copy or reprint portions for
any noncommercial use, except they may not be posted
online without permission. Other permissions will be
reviewed upon request to the Publisher. Request should
be addressed to Permissions - Avoid Student Loans
Green Olive Books, 2159 Glebe Street, Suite 200A,
Carmel, IN 46032.

Interior and Cover Design: Lindsay Hadley

ISBN : 978-0-9834588-0-7

contents

introduction

IT'S SCARY TO HEAR PEOPLE SAY, "THE WORST FINANCIAL DECISION I EVER MADE WAS TO GO TO COLLEGE." YET, THIS PHRASE HAS BECOME MORE AND MORE COMMON. WHY?

There are several reasons for this phenomenon, but the biggest reason is a simple one: student loans. An education that is funded by student loans is an education that could put your financial life at risk. Education is vitally important, but so is financial survival.

The last 18 (or so) years of your life have been filled with images, messages, and suggestions that a college education is the key to a successful and fruitful life. This book isn't about whether or not college is worth your time. This book is about whether or not college is worth money you don't have.

The solution can't be just to give up and forgo your education. The solution is to find a better way to pay for it. You've only heard one side of the student loan story. The story you've heard? If you don't have money saved for college, then student loans are the only way to go. This isn't true. In fact, it's a very dangerous misconception.

There are several ways to lessen the cost of your education. This book details all of them. Some solutions are so simple it will make your head spin. Your willingness to work toward finding college funding solutions now will make your life tremendously easier upon graduation.

One of the most significant steps in lessening your cost of college is the process of applying for and winning scholarships. Many students make the mistake of not even applying for scholarships because they think it is too much work and they don't have a chance to win, or they go in the wrong direction and apply for the same ones as everyone else. They also don't follow a strategy in their scholarship quest and end up wasting time writing many great essays that may create a few close calls, but no real successes.

Instead, these same students turn to student loans to cover their college costs. They hear about the commonality of student loans in the media and popular culture, and what's worse, they see their peers blindly taking them out. Then they take out student loans without even questioning it. Many do this without considering the implications of amassing significant loan debt and how the payments will inhibit their lifestyle after college. You cannot let this be you, under any circumstance.

All of this can be avoided if you follow the advice in this book. We will cover everything from how to make yourself a competitive candidate for scholarship selection, to where to find them and how exactly to win them. The optimal scholarship strategy is distilled into several key steps that will help you succeed. If you follow these steps, we are confident you will significantly decrease the cost of your college education, but most importantly, you will be able to Avoid Student Loans.

Success with scholarships isn't exactly logical and doesn't just come to those with the highest GPAs, those who work the hardest, or those who are the most financially deserving. Scholarship success comes to those who know how the process works and who follow a strategy for winning.

> I spent months writing several essays and filling out countless applications, only to win $1,000 from a committee where I personally knew one of the members.
> **—Aaron**

This book is not about finding scholarships. Any internet search engine can do that. This book is about how to win scholarships. Some of the strategies for winning are intense. They require diligence and getting out of your comfort zone. We ask you throughout the book to form meaningful relationships with people who can assist you with your quest for scholarships. We are **ABSOLUTELY NOT** recommending you form superficial, one-sided relationships. Your ability to find and form relationships will serve you your entire career. This skill is commonly called networking. Not many 18-22 year-olds know how to network properly. Your willingness to learn this skill will greatly improve your chances of winning scholarships.

This book is written for students. If you are a parent reading this text, you too will learn a ton about lessening the cost of college, but only students can best use the book's strategies. Students are the people who are burdened with student loans for a decade or longer. Read the book with your student, and then discuss your strategy together. There is much at stake. You can prevent a financial disaster.

Many of you will read through this book and think it makes sense, yet you won't follow the strategy precisely. You may decide you'd rather just take out unnecessary student loans. We urge you to see the big picture. Do the smart thing, be strategic, and Avoid Student Loans.

Peter and Aaron

chapter 1
College: Is It Truly an Investment?

PRESUMABLY, IF YOU'RE READING THIS BOOK, YOU'VE DECIDED THAT COLLEGE IS A GOOD USE OF YOUR TIME AND (SOMEONE'S) MONEY.

You feel furthering your education will make you a better person, make you a smarter person, and/or make you a more attractive hire upon graduation. All of these ideas may be true. But the most important element in all of this is what you are sacrificing in order to gain this education. What? You didn't know you had to sacrifice something in order to get a college education? You do. No matter who you are, you do.

But here's the good news: you get to choose what you want to sacrifice. And here's the bad news: if you don't choose, then the choice is made for you. And the choice made for you is a terrible one. This book is about helping you make the right choice. Choosing your sacrificial lamb wisely will set you apart from your peers. By following the advice in this book, you will open the door to the perfect financial start to your adult life. You will be the winner.

You will have a college degree. And most importantly, you will have absolutely no student loans.

Think back to when you were eight years old. That seems like a long time ago, right? It was ten years ago, if you are currently 18 years old. So much has changed. Actually, everything has changed. Life's a bit more complicated now. Your eight-year-old self couldn't even begin to understand what your current self is going through. Ten years is a long time. Did you know if you make the wrong choice, you will be paying on your student loans for ten years upon graduation? So if you graduate at age 22, then you will not pay off your four-year college education until you are 32 years old. The decisions you make right now in regards to funding college will affect the next 14 years of your life, if not longer.

According to FinAid.org, 61.1% of four-year public college students borrow money for college, and 70.6% of four-year private college students borrow money for college. You shouldn't look at these numbers and think, "Oh well, everybody's doing it." You are supposed to look at these numbers and think, "How can I avoid being one of those people?" Because if you graduate college without student loans, then you already have a leg up on either 61.1% (public school) or 70.6% (private school) of your peers. While life isn't necessarily about competition, being in a better financial position upon graduation will allow you many more financial options, and having financial options is the goal. Life gets hard when you have very few financial options. You are forced to make choices you don't want to make. By making the right choice now in regards to funding your college education, you eliminate the great option limiter: student loans.

POPULAR SENTIMENT IS WRONG

"It's impossible to go to college without student loans."
- Facebook user post on *Pete the Planner's* fanpage 12/2011.

You must fight the urge to conform to the standards your older brethren have set for you. Yes, student loans are the easiest way to start funding a college education, but this ease quickly disappears. Just like cutting off your legs is the easiest way to lose 60 lbs, the consequences of the easy way out are long lasting. What do you have to gain by accepting the "everybody has student loans truth"? Nothing. Even a moderate amount of student loans is dangerous. In fact, the moderation argument is often times used to justify poor decision making.

For instance, there is a popular sentiment circulating that suggests you should never take out more total student loans than what your first year salary will pay you. As an example, let's say your first year salary upon graduation is $40,000. If you were to follow this popular suggestion, then you would feel comfortable taking student loans up to $40,000. Based on a 5% interest rate and a ten-year payback period, upon graduation your student loan payment would be $424.26 per month. That is 17% of your take-home pay in your first year. (Below you will find the recommended spending percentages for your first year out of college.) That is completely unacceptable. You don't have to put yourself through this. Yet, according to the statistics, over 70% of private school graduates may be faced with this very situation. Say no to all of this garbage. Avoid Student Loans altogether. There's a better a way. There's a smarter way. And you are about to learn it. Don't ruin the first ten years of your life after graduation paying for something you didn't need to borrow money for in the first place. It's ridiculous.

Another often quoted statistic puts the lifetime earnings of a college graduate between $800,000-$1,000,000 higher than someone who only graduated high school. Colleges, student loan providers, and career counselors have pointed to these numbers since they were first gathered in a 2004 study by the College Board. However, a 2010 *Wall Street Journal* article suggests that this reported gap is not as dramatic as the numbers may indicate. Since college inflation continues to outpace general inflation and borrowing has increased significantly, the gap is shrinking. High unemployment has only aggravated the problem. A college education is no longer a ticket to a wonderful financial life. But it can be. It can be if you make the right buying decision.

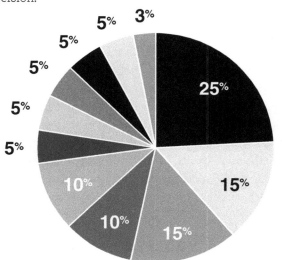

IDEAL
BUDGET

25% Housing ●
15% Transportation
15% Groceries/Dining ●
10% Savings ●
10% Utilities & Phone ●
5% Charity ●
5% Entertainment
5% Medical ●
5% Holidays/Gifts ●
5% Clothing
3% Misc ●

WHAT'S AT STAKE?

Believe it or not, college can ruin your financial life. No one ever tells you this, but it's true. There was a time that you could almost justify your college costs by pointing to the social experience. This poor justification is now ridiculous. You're willing to risk tens of thousands of dollars and over ten years of financial misery for a four year social awakening? (Please say no. Please say no.)

Many students take the seemingly easy way out in paying for college, no matter their motivation for attending. Yet, they are being misled by the government and loan companies into thinking that it's perfectly acceptable to take major loans to cover college expenses. What students don't know is that these loans can have huge negative consequences on their financial futures and make it much more difficult to actually recognize the value and return on the investment of a college degree. Believe it or not, through the use of student loans, we are getting closer to the time when the costs of a college education will outweigh the benefits. That's as painful to write, as it is to read.

> ////////////
> Many students take the seemingly easy way out in paying for college, no matter their motivation for attending. Yet, they are being misled by the government and loan companies into thinking that it's perfectly acceptable to take major loans to cover college expenses.

ASSET OR LIABILITY?

You alone decide whether your college education will be an asset or a liability. You alone decide whether or not your twenties will be burdened with avoidable debt. You alone can begin to create wealth at 18 years old, simply by not taking on liabilities.

If you want to make your college education an asset, then it's important you understand exactly what an asset is. An asset is something you own which has value. And often times an asset provides a return on the initial investment. For instance, you have just acquired an asset by purchasing this book. If you follow the strategy outlined throughout, it will have a return of over 1,000%. Think about it. This book costs about $15. Most small scholarships are at least $1,000, so if you are able to win just one by using what you've learned, you will have paid for this book 66 times over. That is an example of an asset with a very high return on investment.

A liability, on the other hand, is a hindrance. It's something that puts you at a disadvantage. All debts (e.g. mortgages, car loans, student loans) are technically considered liabilities. Owing money to someone or something is a financial hindrance. The debt prevents you from saving money and buying the things you would rather buy.

The real question, however, is this: are you going to get a good return on your investment in your college education? If you fund your college education with student loans, then your chances decrease greatly. College has always been portrayed as an absolute necessity and an asset for your future, but the reality is it can also become a liability depending upon how you pay for it.

The student loan industry wants you to borrow money. That's how they survive. They offer up their services as a solution to an education funding problem. However, their solution actually causes major financial problems upon graduation, which generally last over a decade.

What students don't realize is loans are not the best option. And furthermore, taking them severely increases the time it takes to see a return on your investment in your college education. This book will help prepare you to decrease the initial cost of your education and maximize your scholarships so you can spend less time working, more time studying, and be sure to graduate with a degree that is an asset rather than a liability.

A **liability** is a hindrance. It's something that puts you at a disadvantage. An **asset** is something you own which has value.

STUDENT LOANS CAN ALTER YOUR CAREER PATH

John was a good student in high school, moderately involved in extra-curricular activities, and graduated with a 3.5 GPA. This GPA put him in the top 25% of his graduating class. He attended an in-state university at an estimated cost of $20,000 per year (including tuition, room, and board). His family had a combined household income of $85,000. While this was enough money to comfortably raise a family in one household, it wasn't nearly enough money to also fund a college education. The college he chose disagreed, however, and offered him only $3,000 in financial aid.

His family then filed the FAFSA form and received an expected contribution quote of $17,900, which meant his family was expected to contribute $17,900 to John's education and the government would cover the rest. Unfortunately, the estimated cost of John's education was $17,000 per year (because he received $3,000 in financial aid directly from the university). Therefore, his family was given absolutely no assistance from the government. The government thought that his family could afford $17,900 worth of college expenses on their $85,000 household income.

John and his family then had to come up with a way to get the rest of the money for his education. Combined with his summer employment income, John's family made some major budget cuts and together they were able to collect an additional $5,000. Therefore, John's family had a shortfall of $12,000 annually or $48,000 over the course of his college career, if there was no such thing as college inflation...which, of course, there is.

> Therefore, his family was given absolutely no assistance from the government. The government thought that his family could afford $17,900 worth of college expenses on their $85,000 household income.

John's family felt compelled to turn to student loans. Half of the loans were funded by a student loan from the government at an interest rate of 6.8%, while the other half came from private loans from a local bank at a rate of 8.5%. The loans were repayable over a period of 10 years with a combined payment of $573.76 per month (upon John's graduation from college). For the next 10 years, every month John had to send payment of $573.76 out of his after-tax earnings. This amounted to $6,885.12 per year.

///////////
FAFSA
Free Application for Federal Student Aid

This giant financial obligation placed significant financial stress on John, and it caused him to make some very uncomfortable career decisions. John's primary interests included sports and business, and he felt that he wanted to begin a career in sports marketing. However, the average starting salary in this field is $40,000, and his $48,000 in student loans were a problem. He wasn't able to follow his career aspiration because the education he purchased to pursue his dream was now crushing his dream.

MAKE THE RIGHT CHOICE

It seems incredibly dramatic to indicate that the rest of your life will be affected by your decision to acquire student loans, but it's true. There are many options outside of student loans. Many of these options don't require borrowing money. But all of these options require digging a little deeper for information. Now that you know what's at stake, it's time to Avoid Student Loans.

key takeaways
from chapter 1

1   Student loans are not a necessity.

2   Student loan payments can easily occupy 20% of your take-home pay upon graduation.

3   Loan companies and the government make it seem like loans are a great way to pay for your college, but they aren't.

4   Many students make the mistake of taking loans rather than working to obtain scholarships, and it seriously harms their financial futures.

5   Avoiding student loans opens up more career options for you.

chapter 2

Buy Your Education at a Discount

THINK BACK TO THE LAST TIME YOU SAW A SWEATER YOU WANTED TO BUY. DID YOU BUY IT RIGHT AWAY WITHOUT ASKING TOO MANY QUESTIONS?

If so, then this chapter may save your financial life. Not to ruin your fun shopping for sweaters, but there is a much better way to make a sweater purchase than simply seeing a sweater you like, and then immediately buying it. While you don't have to use the strategy you are about to learn on your clothing purchases, you must use it on your college purchase.

Back to the sweater. Let's assume you find this awesome sweater at your favorite mall retail store, and it's for sale at full retail price. The worst thing you could possibly do is to buy it right now, on the spot. This isn't about being cheap. This is about being smart. You need to do some research.

What should you research? Excellent question. There are many things you should research when making a purchase, no matter if it's a sweater or $100,000 college education.

1 LOOK FOR ALTERNATIVES

Yes, you like that sweater. But what is it about the sweater that you like? Is it the color? The style? Could you get the same amount of satisfaction from another sweater? Again, this isn't meant to take the fun out of life. Actually, this will help you get more out of life. If you can achieve the same satisfaction from a less expensive product, then get the less expensive product.

2 LOOK FOR DISCOUNTS

Will a website have this sweater cheaper? Do you have a relative or friend who works for this store or a similar store and could secure you an employee discount? Does the store offer student discounts?

3 LOOK FOR FREE MONEY

Do you have a gift card that would reduce the cost for you?

AVOID STUDENT LOANS

The entire Avoid Student Loans movement is based on a very simple premise: do everything in your power to Avoid Student Loans. As you read in Chapter one, student loans can be the beginning of the end when it comes to your financial life. There are several ways to Avoid Student Loans, but most students don't even bother to learn what they are. Avoiding student loans takes a focused strategy that should start early in your high school career. While ideally your parents have already set college funds aside for you, often this just isn't the case. It is what it is. Don't waste one minute getting upset about it. Instead, get to work. Exhaust all possibilities. Check out this list of underutilized techniques for reducing the cost of a college education.

TECHNIQUES TO REDUCE THE COST OF YOUR EDUCATION

////////// In some instances, acquiring these college credits while in high school will result in over a 90% discount on tuition.

Earn credits in high school

One of the most significant cost-cutting measures is to secure college credits while you are still in high school. In some instances, acquiring these college credits while in high school will result in over a 90% discount on tuition. You read that right. With early and proper planning, you can eliminate thousands of dollars worth of potential student loans. For instance, at Indiana University there are two different credit hour fee schedules. The first is the credit hour fee schedule for IU Bloomington. It displays the cost of a credit hour for a college student on campus as $263.45 per credit hour. The second is the credit hour fee schedule for Indiana University's ACP (Advance College Project). This is a program that allows high school students to take college courses in various subject areas - for both high school and college credit. According to the schedule, you can gain college credit for just $25 per credit hour. Therefore, you could re-

* http://enrollmentbulletin.indiana.edu/pages/credhrs.php?Term=2
http://acp.indiana.edu/index.php?nodeID=tuitionRateSchedule-generic

ceive 15 credit hours for just $375 via the ACP program. Compare that to the $3,161.40 you would pay as a college student. This strategy alone is worth at least $2786.40. Many high schools and universities across the country have programs similar to this one. It's about time you take a serious look at them.

Earn credits at a less expensive college, and then transfer

Why take your intro courses at expensive institutions when you can take them at inexpensive institutions? It is becoming increasingly popular to attend a community college for the first two years of your college career, and then transfer your credits into a four year college program. Your degree will come from the four year institution, and you will have saved thousands of dollars. You obviously need to check the transfer policy of the four year institution you ultimately would like to graduate from. However, many states have even started to mandate that state schools accept transfer credit from community colleges.
Yes, the government got one right! This technique is perfect for the person who doesn't quite know what he or she wants to study. A general studies degree is still a full price degree... unless you take the first two years worth of classes at a less expensive institution.

Uncle Sam wants YOU

Don't want to bother with scholarships, loans, or less expensive methods for obtaining credit hours? Then join up. Join the military. The GI Bill is one of the most significant things to happen to American education in the last 100 years. Many brave men and women have chosen this route to fund their college educations. A public school education is fully funded under the GI Bill, and a private school education is significantly discounted. The GI Bill benefits are even transferable to some family members. Full details of the program are available at Gibill.va.gov.

Be broke

You should only be broke once in your life. And that time is now. Embrace living frugally. Many a student loan has been used to fund rockstar lifestyles in college. This makes very little sense. Have a great time, but don't try to maintain the same standard of living you had when you lived with your parents. They have an income, you don't. You can either live broke now, or live broke upon graduation when you are supposed to be living well. Rockstar living as a college student almost always leads to pauper living as a graduate. Choose wisely.

///////////

Many a student loan has been used to fund rockstar lifestyles in college. This makes very little sense.

Be smart with textbooks

You do not have to spend thousands of dollars on textbooks. At one point in time, students needed to spend several thousand dollars on overpriced textbooks in order to perform well in college. Websites like Neebo.com and Chegg.com have made it much easier to get the books you need for class at a significant discount. Don't dismiss the importance of obtaining the books you need at an affordable price. It could mean the difference between taking out student loans or not taking out student loans. A complete guide on how to save 50% or more on textbooks is available through the *Avoid Student Loans* Advanced Coaching Program at *AvoidStudentLoans.com.*

Start a profitable business in high school or college
Minimum wage jobs aren't the best for helping you Avoid
Student Loans. If they were, student loans wouldn't be a
problem in this country. So don't get a minimum wage paying
job. Actually, don't get a job at all. Start a business. Some of
the world's top companies were started in college. Facebook,
anyone? Starting a business has endless benefits. You can earn
more money, learn how to operate a business, and put yourself
in a better position to win scholarships. A comprehensive guide
on starting a business to Avoid Student Loans is available at
AvoidStudentLoans.com.

AVOID PARENT LOANS TOO

The solution that isn't a solution is to commit your parents
to paying for your education via parent student loans. Parent
student loans are becoming increasingly popular due to several
factors. As college costs increase and college savings decrease,
parents have begun to choose to take out loans to send their
children to college. In many instances, this is a worse idea
than student loans. If your parents have failed to save for your
education, then there is a degree of likelihood they have also
fallen short in regards to their retirement funding. If these same
parents were to then take out a loan for the next ten years for
your college education, it would severely damage their chances
to retire altogether. There are other methods to fund a college
education. There are not other methods to finance retirement.

THE ULTIMATE SOLUTION

Although evaluating the selection of a particular school, reducing the cost of attendance, and reducing the cost of textbooks is important to Avoid Student Loans, your best bet is to win scholarships. Relax. Don't get bent out of shape. You can win scholarships. And the rest of this book is going to show you exactly how to do it.

Your reluctance to believe you can Avoid Student Loans by winning scholarships is natural, but you need to get over this doubt. You can learn how to win scholarships. And you don't have to be the best student with the best GPA in order to win a scholarship. In fact, here are some things you may not realize:

You don't have to be the best student with the best GPA in order to win a scholarship.

- Many scholarships are won during college, not before.
- Your ability to build relationships on campus can win you scholarships and put your career on the fast track.
- You can't win a scholarship you don't apply for.
- If you want to win a scholarship, you need a great strategy, not necessarily a great high school transcript.

Do you know how to make homemade cinnamon rolls? Do you know how to make the dough? Do you know how much butter, cinnamon, and sugar you should use? Do you know what temperature to bake them at and for how long? You probably don't know any of these things without looking at a recipe. Does that prevent you from making cinnamon rolls on a regular basis? Probably. But who doesn't love cinnamon rolls? For that matter, who doesn't love scholarships. Consider this book one giant recipe...for winning scholarships. If you read this book, and do what it says, then you will be at a distinct advantage when it comes to winning scholarships. The easy choice will bring the worst results. The easy choice is to give up now and acquire student loans. Don't do it. Stand up for your future. Avoid Student Loans.

key takeaways
from chapter 2

1   Don't pay full price for your college education.

2   Saving money on tuition starts in high school.

3   Starting a business in high school or college is better than having a low-paying job.

4   Parent student loans are a worse idea than student loans.

5   Winning scholarships is all about strategy.

chapter 3
/////////
Pay for College With Other People's Money...
Which You Don't Have to Pay Back

ACCORDING TO THE NATIONAL CENTER FOR EDUCATION STATISTICS, NEARLY $3 BILLION IN NON-ATHLETIC SCHOLARSHIPS WERE AWARDED IN 2008.

That's $3 billion in student loans that weren't acquired. The mere mention of the word scholarship makes some people anxious. If you were to ask ten people what their first thought was when hearing the word scholarship, the majority would say something like, "I could never get one." Why is that?

Scholarships are generally classified into two different categories, merit based and need based. A need based scholarship is awarded to people who come from challenging financial backgrounds. This assessment is generally based on your parents' income and assets. Merit based scholarships are based on your awesomeness, whether your awesomeness comes in the form of high academic achievement, or simply being an amazingly well-rounded individual. When people doubt their ability to earn a scholarship it's either because they think their parents earn too much money, or because they don't believe they are deserving. If your parents make "too much money" then you won't win need based scholarships. But that doesn't mean that you should abandon your scholarship quest altogether. Instead, you should focus on perfecting and then highlighting your awesomeness. Does this sound strange? It's not. Here is the story of Aaron Martin, co-author of this book.

AARON'S STORY

My family has always placed a high value on a college degree. And they believe a college degree is exponentially more valuable when it is paid for by the attendee. While my parents did offer to help pay for college, I decided I didn't want to place this burden on them. But more importantly, I was up for the challenge of trying to pay for my own college education. The catch? I refused to take out student loans. My strategy was simple: win as many scholarships as I could.

WHAT I WAS WORKING WITH

My high school GPA was solid, but not good enough to compete for the top scholarships based on GPA and/or SAT/ACT scores. And although I had a variety of extracurricular interests, I was not deeply involved with many extracurriculars because I didn't want to dedicate all of my time and effort to just one activity.

///////////
I refused to take out student loans. My strategy was simple: win as many scholarships as I could.

I continued exploring and looking for something of interest to me. I was always interested in business and began daydreaming about running my own business. Ultimately these visions paid off. I realized starting my own business was the perfect way to begin paying for my college education. My family lived near a reservoir filled with boats every summer. However, the strange thing was there weren't many boat related service businesses in the area. This was my chance.

I did some research and discovered I could start a mobile detailing business with a small initial investment. After a few months of planning and hard work, the business became profitable. My determination to pay for my own college education, combined with my interest in business, helped me earn thousands of dollars to pay for my education. So while some of my peers were stressed with their involvements and commitments, I was having fun, making money, and learning more about one of my major interests. I realized even though I was just a teenager, a good business idea is a good business idea. I didn't

Pay for College With Other People's Money...Which You Don't Have to Pay Back

let older adults convince me I wasn't qualified to run a success-ful business. I believed in myself, I worked hard, and I set the groundwork for paying for my own college education. However, little did I know this spark of entrepreneurship would also be the catalyst for winning several thousand dollars in scholarships.

SCHOLARSHIP TIME

The experience of running my own business proved useful when scholarship time rolled around. As I previously mentioned, my main strategy for paying for my own college education was twofold: to avoid student loans and to win scholarships. In the fall of my senior year in high school as my classmates and I began to apply to college, the guidance counselors at my school encouraged everyone to fill out a general application for a list of 30 scholarships and to check the usual scholarship websites. It seemed reasonable at the time. These were professionals. Their job was to help me get to college, and to help me pay as little in student loans as possible. Or so I thought. Only later did I realize how ineffective this process was.

"File your FAFSA, so that you can see how much aid you can get based on your parents' income. And apply for these scholarships."

While this advice seemed helpful at first glance, it wasn't. I knew the list of 30 scholarships. I wanted to win. I wanted the counselors to teach me how to win these scholarships. They didn't do this. But ultimately, I don't blame them. It wasn't their job to teach me how to win scholarships. So I learned on my own.

I initially followed the counselors' advice and applied for the standard list of scholarships offered by the school. I ended up spending many hours on this process, only to win $1,000. This wasn't going to work. I needed a strategy.

I decided to think like a businessman. My boat detailing business was based on relationships. I knew my customers well, and they knew me well. They referred me to their friends because they liked me, and wanted to see my business flourish.

> "File your FAFSA, so that you can see how much aid you can get based on your parents' income. And apply for these scholarships."

Relationships work like that. The acquaintances you make, whether during business or pleasure, want to see you succeed. I had figured out my strategy. I needed relationships.

MY WINNING STRATEGY

My goal was to pay for my own college education. My method was to use scholarships instead of student loans. My strategy was to develop meaningful relationships with people who could help me accomplish my goal. There was no time to waste. I needed to get to know the right people.

I selected the university I wanted to attend, and I got right to work. Prior to even applying for admission to the university, I scheduled a meeting with the honors program coordinator of the business school. I headed to campus, took a tour, and met with her to express my sincere enthusiasm for this prestigious school. I was polite and direct. I told her about my experiences in high school, my business, and I mentioned I was seeking to maximize my scholarship aid since I was paying for my college education on my own. Throughout my senior year I saw the coordinator, as well as other advisors, at several recruiting events. Maintaining contact with these individuals was key. I developed the relationships early and began to build my reputation as a student who wanted to come to the school, maximize the value of my education, and make the most of my efforts and involvement. I stood out as being confident, personable, and valuable to the school.

I had built a brand. A brand is your reputation, but so much more. It's your style, your consistency, and your personality. Businesses spend millions of dollars trying to build consistent brands. So why shouldn't a prospective college student spend several hours trying to build his or hers? This is exactly what I did. And this is exactly what you should do too.

After I was accepted to the university, my initial contact with the honors program coordinator allowed the scholarship committee to recognize my name when it came time to allocate awards. This happened because I had developed a brand and

> I had built a brand. A brand is your reputation, but so much more. It's your style, your consistency, and your personality.

had expressed interest and commitment to the school I wanted to attend. My efforts resulted in several thousand dollars in scholarships from the school. I also visited another honors division of the university and scheduled meetings with some of their key people. I was able to earn an additional scholarship of a few thousand dollars from this group, all by conveying my enthusiasm and dedication to my education.

From these initial meetings with university coordinators and professors, I secured over ten times the amount of scholarship money that I did applying for the list of scholarships my high school handed me.

SNOWBALL EFFECT

I became addicted. I kept thinking, "You're telling me that building meaningful relationships with important people could help me pay for college?" The more networking I did, the more my confidence grew. The more my confidence grew, the more scholarships I won. Talking with professors and previous winners led me to more and more opportunities. Without a doubt, one of the most important lessons I learned was the power of asking. When you put yourself in the right position, asking for guidance can be powerful. There is no downside to asking. The worst thing that can happen is for someone to say "no." But who cares if they do say "no"? You never had what you were asking for in the first place.

I also learned the importance of having the information advantage. Know everything. Know who won the scholarship last year. Know who awards the scholarship. And know every detail about the process. Don't just apply and hope that someone gives you free money. Earn it with your efforts. This book will teach you exactly how to do that. It will give you a path to follow to Avoid Student Loans and maximize your scholarship earnings.

> "You're telling me that building meaningful relationships with important people could help me pay for college?"

Below are the processes I followed to win not one, but two of the most prestigious scholarships on my campus.

WORKING STUDENT SCHOLARSHIP

This scholarship was for students who were working to pay for a portion of their college education via their employment income. It covered a large amount of attendance costs, but it also was one of the most competitive on campus. The winner would exemplify not only an outstanding character, but also a commitment to education, community, and their future. It required tax statements as proof of income, several recommendation letters and essays, as well as a comprehensive application and interview process.

I knew several people who were interested in this scholarship, but they didn't want to go through all of the effort to gather the materials to apply. I knew, however, that if I went about it strategically, I would definitely have a shot at winning.

Pay for College With Other People's Money...Which You Don't Have to Pay Back

Here's exactly how I won:

Step 1:
Called scholarship administrator to discuss the qualities and past experiences of current winners and obtain their contact information

Step 2:
Researched on the scholarship, its requirements, and the man who it's named for, mainly his career and life experiences

Step 3:
Contacted past winner and scheduled a lunch to discuss her strategy, essay content, and structure

Step 4:
Wrote application and essay with ease because I had background knowledge on winning essay structures

Step 5:
Obtained outstanding recommendation letters by providing the letter writers a document highlighting my specific experiences and skills

Step 6:
Turned in all materials in person, and followed up with the administrator by thanking her for the opportunity to apply

Step 7:
Prepared for my interview with the committee by mapping out interesting conversations and practicing interview questions

Step 8:
Followed up on the interview by emailing the committee members, thanking them for their time, reminding them why the scholarship was so important to me, and emphasizing how the scholarship would further my progress in reaching my goals

Step 9:
Wrote thank you notes to everyone involved, after being informed I won the scholarship

ENTREPRENEURSHIP SCHOLARSHIP

This scholarship was for students who were committed to entrepreneurship and who had expressed interest in owning their own business someday. It was endowed by a very successful entrepreneur who valued "go-getters" and was to be awarded to a student who was planning on putting his or her education to use by starting a business. The application required essays on past entrepreneurial experiences, interviews, and a recommendation letter.

And just like the Working Student Scholarship, I won. Here is my winning strategy:

Step 1:
Learned about this hard-to-find scholarship through a meeting with the previous winner

Step 2:
Researched scholarship background and the entrepreneur who created it

Step 3:
Scheduled a meeting with a committee member and developed a meeting agenda highlighting things of importance to him, as well as my entrepreneurial experience and future plans

Step 4:
Met with the committee member, took notes during meeting, shared my ideas, and asked for a book recommendation

Step 5:
Told my entrepreneurial story, starting the boat detailing business, and discussed future plans through the essays

Step 6:
Read the book the committee member recommended, attended the events he was involved with on campus, and followed up with him the week before the application process was closed

Step 7:
Interviewed with the committee

Step 8:
Followed up with the committee after the interview and thanked them for their time and consideration, emphasizing how this scholarship would help me progress as an entrepreneur

Step 9:
Wrote thank you notes to all involved, after being informed I had won the scholarship.

YOU CAN DO IT TOO

While my strategy was intelligent, my scholarship winnings had nothing to do with my intelligence. I won because of my strategy. You can replicate and build on these successes. Ultimately, I covered the majority of the cost of my education through these scholarships, and others, because I was strategic and persistent. Anyone can be strategic and persistent. It's just a matter of choice.

Pay for College With Other People's Money...Which You Don't Have to Pay Back

key takeaways
from chapter 3

Pay for College With Other People's Money...Which You Don't Have to Pay Back

1 Your reluctance to apply for scholarships is natural, but you need to get over it.

2 There are two types of scholarships, need based and merit based.

3 You can win scholarships by having a great strategy.

4 Scholarship success has a snowball effect.

5 You must make a compelling case to the scholarship committee members.

chapter 4

Build Your Story to Stand Out From the Crowd

HAVING A GREAT STORY TO TELL IS THE KEY TO DIFFERENTIATING YOURSELF FROM THE OTHER CANDIDATES. WHEN IT COMES DOWN TO IT, IT'S NOT YOUR GPA OR TITLES THAT MATTER, BUT HOW YOU PRESENT YOURSELF. //////////////

Why is Starbucks able to charge so much for a cup of coffee? Is it because their coffee is better than their competitors' coffee? Probably not. Simply put, they have a better brand. They have told a better story. This doesn't make them dishonest. This doesn't make them sneaky. This makes them smart. They market themselves better than their competitors. People like them and find them comforting. People feel at ease when they walk into a Starbucks. You need to be the Starbucks of the scholarship application world.

The tough reality is most scholarship applicants will have similar activities and qualifications to you. Your application, if you don't use strategy, will look exactly the same as most of the other candidates' applications. That's why you must differentiate yourself. You cannot allow yourself to be grouped together with the other applicants. You must stand out from your peers. Your grades might not allow you to do so, but don't fret. There's another way to go about this, a better way.

With a good story, and passion for your life and future plans, you can easily stand out against anyone with a better GPA and more involvement; it's simply about convincing the committee you are the most deserving candidate through telling a better story and being memorable.

DON'T BE A FIGUREHEAD, BE A DIFFERENCE MAKER

Achievements that seem meaningful, sometimes aren't in the scholarship world. For instance, it's not unique to say you were an officer in a club or an organization. Many applicants will have these leaderships roles. But what can be unique is the story you tell about your accomplishments while in that position. It's best to focus on actions and results rather than titles. A "member" of a club who organized her peers to come together to raise $1,000 and help clean up the yards of the elderly has a much better story than an officer who scheduled meetings and did paperwork. On the other hand, the officer could tell a story about how she, through leading the meetings, created the opportunity for people to collaborate and volunteer as a group, while raising money at the same time. Therefore, it's all about your perspective and ability to articulate the results you feel the committee will value.

Scholarship committees generally look for three things:

1. You started something new or did something different.
2. You had great success in something with which you were involved.
3. You applied the knowledge you acquired through your education to accomplish something outside of the classroom.

A story including one or more of these three ideas will make a great impression on the committee. Try to think how you can apply one of these three concepts to your experiences.

HIGHLIGHT YOUR UNIQUENESS

Uniqueness can't be manufactured. But it can be highlighted. Can't think of any place where your unique talents shine? Then find a need, and fill it in with your skill set. Consider an emerging interest among students of your high school or university. Is there an opportunity to start an organization to bring these students together? Need another idea? Think of a business need on your campus or elsewhere, and then get to work. These two ideas demonstrate your initiative. Your confidence and ambition will speak loudly to the scholarship committee.

If you are already involved with a certain organization you love, take on a project that will make a valuable contribution to this group, or simply plan an event for your organization. It's through these opportunities that you will be able to learn and grow the most, and will be able demonstrate your dedication and creativity.

Ultimately, your ability to highlight your uniqueness is driven by your willingness to be a meaningful member of the community in which you live. You can be a member of every extracurricular program on the planet, but if you don't contribute anything to these groups or to the community, then you will never be able to differentiate yourself from your peers. If you take an active role, you will have a great amount to talk about, and also grow significantly as a person.

Ultimately, your ability to highlight your uniqueness is driven by your willingness to be a meaningful member of the community in which you live.

INVOLVEMENT: QUALITY OVER QUANTITY

It is much better to participate in one or two activities outside of the classroom, rather than five which you can't really dedicate yourself to because you are being pulled in various directions. All selection committees agree the quality of your involvement is much more important than the quantity of your involvements. When you truly dedicate yourself to a few activities, you have many more opportunities to gain valuable experiences, which you can discuss in interviews and write about in essays.

SETTING CAREER GOALS HELPS YOU TELL YOUR STORY

When building your story, it is important to find something which you can apply your skills to and where you will learn a great deal. This will help you determine where you want to be in the future, but more importantly, it will help you develop specific goals. Goals are the key to success not only in the professional world, but in the scholarship world as well. It takes considerable effort and thought to develop goals, but your effort will be rewarded. Goals give you your own personal path to success. When you set goals, your mind begins to create solutions.

For instance, if you establish a goal to be one of the world's top heart surgeons in the future, then you should begin to think of activities you can do to put yourself closer to achieving this goal. If you don't know where you are going, then you will never get where you want to be, so it is important to establish goals to help you toward your dreams. However, if you don't have a clear picture of what you want to do for a living, you can use that to your advantage too. Simply tell the story of how you tried a little bit of everything to try to find your passion. This can make for a great story, if you tell it correctly, by emphasizing what you've learned along the way and how you have grown from each of the different experiences.

> Goals are the key to success not only in the professional world, but in the scholarship world as well. It takes considerable effort and thought to develop goals, but your effort will be rewarded.

 **HERE ARE THE FOUR QUESTIONS TO ASK YOURSELF WHEN TRYING TO ESTABLISH CAREER GOALS FOR THE VERY FIRST TIME:**

1.   What sort of lifestyle do you want to be living in 10-20 years?

2.   What is something you enjoy doing that doesn't feel like work, even though it is?

3.   What were your favorite childhood pastimes (i.e. building things, drawing, working outdoors, etc.)?

4.   How can you combine these things in a way that allows you to provide value to others, and allows you to earn a living?

Answering these questions allows you to find a possible career path that plays to your interests, but better yet, allows you to tell a personal story of why you want to get there.

MAXIMUM IMPACT AND RESULTS

Once you identify a goal you are passionate about, you must then think of how you can work your way towards it. For example, if you have a part-time job you enjoy, think of something you can get out of that experience that will help prepare you for reaching your future goals. If you aspire to be a successful business person, this experience might be shadowing the owner or top executive of the company you work for. Shadowing would provide valuable material for a great story, and it would be a very educational experience outside your everyday responsibilities. You need to think differently than other people. You need to see opportunities in everyday situations.

In whatever activity you choose, seek to make the maximum impact possible. Don't just be a member, find an important role so you can contribute even if there is no title attached. Titles don't matter; it's the experience and what you do with it that matters. Below are two progression charts of involvement for people who are focused on their goals.

///////// *Student interested in foreign affairs*

| took foreign language | studied international business | raised money to fund trip | traveled to dream country | met with influential foreign leader |

///////// *Student interested in entrepreneurship*

| worked part time | learned about business | researched opportunities | developed business plan | started small business |

Both of these people established their goals and took steps to achieve them. This creates a good story for them to tell about their experiences and all they learned along the way. It also shows their drive to succeed because they identified something they wanted to do and took the right actions to get there.

TELL YOUR STORY

Now that you have chosen the right involvement suited to your passions and interests, it is important to articulate it in the optimal way. When telling your story, it is best to use a proven strategy called the STAR method. It works like this:

STAR Method

SITUATION	Give example of situation you were involved in that had a positive outcome
TASK	Describe the tasks involved in that situation
ACTIONS	Talk about the various actions involved in the situation's tasks
RESULTS	Identify the results from your actions

When telling your story, use specific examples and highlight the skills you used and what you learned from the experiences.

Example of a STAR Answer

SITUATION	During my summer internship, I was responsible for managing several events
TASK	I noticed attendance had been dropping and wanted to do something to improve it.
ACTIONS	I designed a new promotional campaign and developed a feedback assessment on our events to determine customer satisfaction improvement opportunities.
RESULTS	We utilized the ideas we received from past customers, improved our experience, and raised attendance by 15% during my internship.

//////////
If you distinguish yourself by working hard, you will find that other opportunities will keep coming your way. It is up to you to take advantage of these unexpected opportunities.

THE PURPOSE OF HAVING A PURPOSE

Often what scholarship committees look for is to see if you have a purpose, and more importantly, to see if you are motivated to achieve your goals. Therefore, it is important to establish your goals from the beginning, and take action toward achieving them. When telling your story, if you highlight your passion and show how you are pursuing it, you will be a much stronger candidate than one who simply talks about what he or she has accomplished. The key is in relating your accomplishments to your passion. When you show you have purpose and goals you are working towards and can tell the story of how your actions relate to that goal, you will be miles ahead of the other candidates. This is one of the biggest secrets of avoiding student loans through maximizing your scholarships. Establish your goals, take effective action towards achieving them through involvement on and off campus, and tactfully let others know about it.

SOCIAL MEDIA IS NOT YOUR FRIEND

Whereas social media (Facebook, Twitter, MySpace, Tumblr, etc.) is a fun way to interact with your friends, it can destroy your chances at a scholarship. Your behavior, ideas, photos, and images are all captured online via your social media profiles. That inappropriate tweet, that purposefully misspelled rude Facebook status update, and that awkward article that you posted to Tumblr, can wipe away all your hard work with just one view. This isn't only true for your attempt to earn scholarships, but this will ring true throughout your professional life.

Upon receiving your completed scholarship application, more and more scholarship committees are turning to Google to eliminate candidates for scholarships. A simple Google search of your name will turn up your social media profiles. This is where things can potentially go horrifically wrong. It just takes one curse word (or something worse) to convince a committee member you aren't the right person to represent the scholarship.

Use the "Grandma Rule." Don't ever post anything that you wouldn't show your grandma. Many careers have been ruined because of inappropriate social media use. Follow the "Grandma Rule" and you can't go wrong, unless your grandma happens to be the "coolest" grandma on the planet.

////////

USE THE "GRANDMA RULE"
Don't ever post anything that you wouldn't show your grandma.

key takeaways
from chapter 4

//////////////

1   Great experiences lead to great lessons and stories.

2   A great story is the key to winning over a committee, being remembered, and winning scholarships.

3   Use the STAR Method when telling your story.

4   Focus on quality of involvement over quantity.

5   Have a purpose, establish goals, and work to achieve them.

6   Inappropriate social media use can cost you tens of thousands of dollars in scholarships.

part 2

Networking to Find and Win Scholarships

////////////////

This section covers the key aspects of finding lucrative opportunities through utilizing the knowledge of people who are in the know and willing to help you.

chapter 5

Find the Winners

WHILE IT'S IMPORTANT TO FOLLOW THE FRAMEWORK LAID OUT IN THIS BOOK, YOU ALSO NEED TO FIND PEOPLE ON YOUR CAMPUS WHO HAVE ACHIEVED SUCCESS WITH SCHOLARSHIPS. ////////

They will be able to provide more personalized advice, specific to your particular campus, as well as introductions to certain people of influence.

Imagine you are at a carnival. You are on the hunt for your favorite carnival food, a funnel cake. You've been walking around the carnival for nearly two hours, and yet, you haven't found the funnel cake stand. Just as you are about to abandon all hope, a guy walks by with a funnel cake. What do you do? You ask him where he got the funnel cake! You ask him how he got there and how you can too.

As you learned in high school geometry, the shortest distance between two points is a straight line. If you want information on how to win a particular scholarship, then you need to go directly to the right source: the person who previously won it. But in all likelihood, you don't know this person. This is why you need to learn how to network.

If you learn only one skill from this book, it needs to be how to network. If you learn to network effectively, not only will you win scholarships, but you will establish relationships that will continue to help you throughout your career. Your network is the group of people you develop relationships with, but more importantly, your network also includes the people your friends know. This is one of the great secrets to success. You are only one step away from possibly meeting the person who could change your career. That important introduction could come through a current friend. It's like Facebook, in a way. The "suggested friends" section points you toward people your friends already know. Your ability to develop and leverage these relationships could mean the difference between career success and underachievement. So, in addition to your primary goal of winning scholarships, one of your secondary focuses must be building networks.

///////////
Why do you think your grandpa loves to talk your ear off and give you constant advice? Because he has experienced a lot in his lifetime and wants to share with you the wisdom he has acquired.

LEVERAGE THE EXPERIENCE OF OTHERS

When you build up your network you leverage the knowledge and experience of others. The second best thing to knowing everything, is knowing someone who knows what you want to know. When people amass experiences over the course of their lifetime, they filter their findings down to specific insights of wisdom they readily and happily share with others, when given the opportunity. You need to be there to receive the knowledge they want to share.

Why do you think your grandpa loves to talk your ear off and give you constant advice? Because he has experienced a lot in his lifetime and wants to share with you the wisdom he has acquired.

Now, you're probably wondering how this relates to avoiding student loans and winning scholarships. Well, think about it. If you knew someone who had won many scholarships, do you think he would be able to recognize the specific method that led to his success, and tell you how to do the same? Of course he would!

Most likely, there are several students on your campus who have figured out how to play the game. Often, they are not even the brightest or most involved students, yet they know what works to get the scholarships on your particular campus. They have been through the process of preparing themselves to be good candidates, searching for the scholarships, applying for them, and ultimately winning them, and they can provide you with the insight you need to succeed. You just have to find them!

INSIDE INFORMATION

These winners will have the inside information you need to know when seeking to maximize your scholarships and fund your education the right way.

Experienced winners know where to find the scholarships, as well as the specifics on what types of scholarships are most infrequently won so you can avoid these. They will have knowledge of the little-known scholarships where you will have a much better chance of winning. In addition, they will be able to guide your search for the best scholarships to consider for your particular situation.

Furthermore, these winners will be able to recommend how to best prepare yourself for the scholarship competition. They are likely well-connected around campus and know what involvement is effective and influential and what isn't. So, they will be able to advise you accordingly as to how to make yourself stand out for a particular scholarship opportunity.

These past winners will be able to tell you what to write in your essays and say in the interviews, as well as how to tailor your application to highlight your specific experiences and skill sets. They have gone through this process before you and know what needs to be said.

Most importantly, however, they will have knowledge of the faculty and administration in charge of the scholarships you are looking for. They will be able to tell you whom to talk with, what you need to say to them, as well as how to build good relationships with these people who will be critical in your success both in your scholarship quest and in your college career.

Now, you're probably wondering, isn't that why I bought this book, to learn what works? Yes, and this book is giving you the principles of what works and the framework you need to follow. However, using your specific network and modeling successful people on your specific campus will provide a personalized approach. This guide can't tell you who specifically to talk to, or what scholarships are the most underrated and overpaying; nevertheless, it can give you the framework for success. It's up to you to pull everything together.

The approach of leveraging the existing knowledge of others applies across a variety of fields from engineering to medicine to education, and it most certainly applies to your quest to maximize scholarship earnings. When you stand on the shoulders of those who have come before you, you elevate yourself to heights you never thought possible, like finding a way to avoid student loans and win more scholarships.

FIND THE KEY PEOPLE AND GET THEIR ATTENTION

It is important to locate the people who have had success with scholarships and to connect with them. At times these students may be hard to find because they are likely some of the people you'd least expect. Most are not the presidents and founders of organizations, but those who quietly indulge their own interests, enjoy their time, and have outside pursuits.

PAY IT FORWARD

Often a sense of individuality helped these past winners succeed in the first place. You might be thinking, why would someone like this want to connect with me?

Don't worry, they will. It's human nature to want to talk
about past successes. There is nothing for these past winners to
lose, as they have already secured their winnings, so there's no
downside to sharing their methodology with you.

Paying it forward is very important, and when people who
have achieved success see others trying to make their own way,
something ignites inside them and they want to help in any way
they can. They have fond memories of their "struggle" and want
to help others get on the right path as well.

Often the founders and CEOs of top companies will be
more than willing to make time in their busy schedules to see
a hot prospect, an up-and-comer who has made the effort to
secure a meeting. The same applies in this situation. Someone
who has excelled in obtaining scholarships would love to talk
about his story and help you. Winning scholarships has given
this person great pleasure and he more than likely wants to
provide this same opportunity to others.

///////////////////////////

Networking led to this book: it never
would have been written without
networking. Aaron, a young guy
looking to make his mark, randomly
emailed Pete, a young guy who had
already made his mark in the media,
writing, and online. Ten years ago
Pete used to randomly contact
business leaders when he was trying
to learn how to network. He still asks
for meetings from people he doesn't
know, but would like to know. Aaron
started doing this in high school,
and he continues still today.

LEVERAGE THE EXPERIENCE OF OTHERS

The first step is to call the office of the school and ask to speak with a scholarship manager or an honors academic advisor. If you can't talk with this person on the phone, schedule an appointment because it will be worth it, and these people are often very busy. Ask this advisor if he or she knows of anyone who has been particularly successful in obtaining scholarship winnings. Honors advisors work with the top students on campus, and these former winners often subtly talk about their successes with the right people. Academic advisors and scholarship managers frequently come into contact with these students or hear their names mentioned, and thus have a familiarity with these students.

Try to obtain a list of the top five to ten juniors and seniors who have achieved success with scholarships, and get their email addresses.

////////////
Try to obtain a list of the top five to ten juniors and seniors who have achieved success with scholarships, and get their email addresses.

PERSISTENCE PAYS

Persist until you succeed in obtaining the contact information you need. If the first person you encounter can't help you, ask her if she knows someone who can, and continue this until you find the right people. It will be worth it. Your persistence will pay off.

Other people you will want to get into contact with are the scholarship or disbursement coordinators of your university's foundation. These officials are in charge of managing and disbursing the donations of your university's endowment fund. They are knowledgeable about which scholarships are available and how to go about obtaining them. Additionally, they have lists of current winners they could give you so that you can connect with these people. Many officials will tell you to just look on their website, however, this is not a good method because it's what everyone else does. Your personal interaction with these officials is important. They need to know your name.

If you've exhausted your efforts in getting this information from the scholarship officials, then you need to turn to the Internet. Look on the foundation website, or do a Google search with terms like "(Name of college)+foundation+scholarships."

Searches of this type can help you narrow down specific scholarships and the winners you need to contact. This is a different approach than simply going through the scholarship sites like everyone does. Remember, to achieve uncommon results like being paid to go to school, you must take the uncommon path!

To find the contact information of past winners, either search for them on Facebook with your university selected, or obtain it through the honors advisor or professors they might interact with.

The key is being persistent because it is highly likely that once you get into contact with these people, they will be more than willing to help you.

> Remember, to achieve uncommon results like being paid to go to school, you must take the uncommon path!

THE INITIAL EMAIL

When you connect with previous winners the first time, you want your contact to be fairly formal. This is why you should avoid sending a Facebook message. The best method of engagement is email. The key is to write a tactful and polite email that expresses your need directly and your desire to connect with them. The email should be short, to the point, have a purpose, and end with an action suggestion such as scheduling a meeting.

Below are comparisons of good and bad emails.

A BAD EMAIL WILL RUIN YOUR CHANCES

////////////////

Eric,

I heard you have won many scholarships on campus and I want to figure out how to do that.

NEGATIVES
////////////

1 Too short
2 Appears self-centered
3 Doesn't build connection
4 Reader will be likely to discard because it is impersonal

I want a lot of financial assistance and would like you to tell me how you got it so I can too.

What can you do to help me out?
Thanks,
Brian Smith
bsmith@auniversity.edu ////////////////

A GOOD EMAIL CAN MAKE ALL THE DIFFERENCE

Hello Eric,
My name is Brian Smith and I am a freshman at
A University studying business. I heard from my advisor,
Amanda Hill, that you have enjoyed lots of success with
scholarships, and she recommended I contact you.

I am in the process of applying for several and know you
would be the right person to consult for some guidance.
I would value hearing your story about how you obtained
so many scholarships and would appreciate your advice
on how to achieve my own success.

Would you be willing to meet for lunch at College Café on
campus sometime next week? I'm buying! The best days for
me are Tuesdays and Thursdays in the time range of 11-1.

Thanks, and I look forward to the opportunity to meet and
discuss this with you.

Sincerely,
Brian Smith
bsmith@auniversity.edu)

POSITIVES

1 Introduces yourself
2 Makes common connection
3 Explains why you want to talk
4 Expresses value and appreciation
5 Treats the person to lunch
6 Makes it easy to schedule a meeting
7 Thanks the person and expresses enthusiasm about the chance to meet
8 Provides contact information

The key when writing an email is to think from the perspective of the person who will be reading it. If you pretend you are that person, think how you would feel if you received the email and whether or not you would be willing to reply and meet for lunch.

The good email connects with the reader and feels complimentary to him, while the bad email voices the self-serving attitude of "what's in it for me?"

INITIAL MEETING AND DISCUSSION

If you contact a few people successful with scholarships, you will be likely to schedule at least a lunch or two. This hour of time is extremely valuable if used properly because you can gather all kinds of useful information while there. The key is to come prepared with a list of general questions, as well as a few specific ones about any major scholarship opportunities you have heard about at this point.

Below is a suggested list of questions and discussion points:

General

How did you find out about your scholarships?

Were there specific people you connected with regarding them?

What did you do to prepare yourself?

What was the application and selection process like?

What do you feel was the major disadvantage of the other candidates?

What activities are you involved in on campus?

Specific
////////////

Which faculty members should I contact regarding this scholarship?

Do you know others who have won an extensive amount of scholarships?

What should I say to the faculty members in an interview situation?

Is there anything specific the committee is looking for in the essay?

Make sure you are socially acceptable when meeting with a past winner. Greet her with a firm handshake and steady eye contact, thank her for taking the time to talk with you, and don't make a big deal out of paying for her lunch. It will cost about $10, which will be made back over 100 times if you win even the smallest scholarship as a result of her advice.

End the meeting by thanking her again and asking if she would be willing to follow up by reviewing your application materials or letting you read hers. You will likely need to write multiple essays, and it would be very beneficial if you had a copy of one of her past essays or at least her help in reviewing yours.

Don't push the issue of getting a copy of her essay, however. If she is unwilling to give you a copy just ask her if she would look over your essay and offer specific advice on how to improve it via email. After the lunch, be sure to send a follow-up email and thank her for her time and advice.

////////////
Make sure you are socially acceptable when meeting with a past winner. Greet her with a firm handshake and steady eye contact, and thank her for taking the time to talk with you.

NETWORKING IS ESSENTIAL

You've just learned to network effectively. Some people never learn this skill. It takes practice to perfect. The more you do it, the better you will get at it. You will quickly learn that people are very willing to help you, as long as you graciously ask for their help. You will know when you are a good networker when people start trying to network with you. Be sure to make it easy on them. Someone is going to help you, and you need to be sure to return the favor.

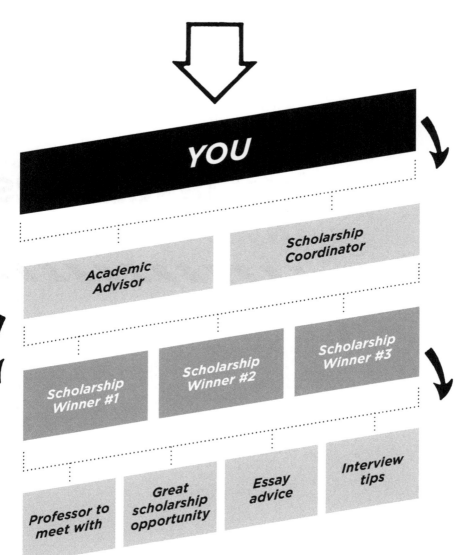

key takeaways
from chapter 5

1   Open yourself up to the generosity
     of others willing to give advice, and
     find the right people to connect with.

2   Take action. Make the phone calls,
     schedule the meetings, and ask the
     right questions.

3   Be personable and communicate
     effectively and clearly both in person
     and in your emails.

4   Act on former winners' advice,
     follow-up with the people they
     recommend you meet and look for the
     scholarships they direct you toward.

5   Pay it forward and help others in the
     future when they come to you.

chapter 6

Network With Influential People

WE'VE ALL HEARD THE SAYING, IT'S NOT WHAT YOU KNOW, BUT WHO YOU KNOW. THIS IDIOM APPLIES TO THE SCHOLARSHIP WORLD, AND THE SOONER YOU GET IN THE GAME, THE BETTER YOUR CHANCES FOR SUCCESS.

//////////////

****IMPORTANT AUTHOR'S NOTE**

The following chapter is very important. But it is also very dangerous if executed inappropriately. This chapter will teach you how to network with very influential individuals in an appropriate way.

Do not misinterpret the process. The aim is to form sincere, meaningful relationships with people who can help you achieve your goals. The aim is not to use people in order to get what you want. This is a very fine line. *Proceed cautiously.*

When determining scholarship winners, the final decision often comes down to only a few committee members, but these primary decision makers gather the opinions of many to help form their decision. Therefore, it's either important to know the committee members directly, or know someone influential whom they are likely to consult for a recommendation. It's essential to be known by influential people and have them hold you in high regard. This is the secret not only to obtaining the best scholarships, but also to enriching your college experience. It can even give you a great start to your career. The more people who know and think highly of you, the more amazing opportunities you will find.

//////////////

CREATE A PRISTINE REPUTATION

Your reputation results from sincere, genuine, and purposeful actions. This isn't about being fake. Be impressive. And then gain a reputation for being impressive. It's important to be known across your campus or within your program as a person of influence and as an achiever with potential.

GET STRATEGICALLY INVOLVED

The simplest and most effective way to get involved is to actually go to class, pay attention, and participate. By paying attention and actively listening, you gain the respect of your professors, which is a key step in building a good reputation. It's not hard to put the cell phone and laptop away for a few hours each day and focus on your professors. And the added benefit is you can cut your study time in half because you absorb the material much better during the class.

Your reputation is the most valuable asset you have; therefore, it is important to enhance and protect it.

It also isn't difficult to raise your hand every once in awhile to ask or answer a question. Making it a point to speak once, at least every other class, takes minimal effort but will put you in an elite category in your professor's mind. If you watch, the majority of your classmates will not participate, so in raising your hand, you stand out. Attracting the attention of your professors is essential because they are in the position to recommend you for scholarships, and in addition, a selection committee could potentially consult them in the scholarship decision making process.

Another great way to become effectively involved on campus is to speak with your advisor and ask about how you can help with info sessions, prospective student tours, orientation programs, and extra-curricular events. Many faculty and administrators are required to attend these events, and as a volunteer you have the opportunity to work alongside them and form a relationship, or at least become a familiar face.

Consider this scenario: there are two final candidates interviewing with a scholarship committee. A few weeks ago, several of the committee members worked at a freshman orientation program and saw Candidate A there volunteering for an hour. They never saw Candidate B. The committee members will likely remember Candidate A because they saw him taking his own time to help the school. This is a competitive advantage for Candidate A. Why not put yourself in this position?

Countless activities occur around your school you can get involved with. From appreciation lunches with alumni and donors to special selective learning programs, these are all opportunities to build your reputation as someone who cares about the community. If you seek and obtain admission to one of these programs, or find a way to get yourself invited to an alumni lunch, you will become a familiar face to the faculty who attend such events and will develop profitable and enjoyable relationships with them.

HALLWAY CONVERSATION

If you spend enough time walking around your school, you are bound to run into your professors and other administrators in the hallways. This is a chance for a quick hello, and when time permits, a brief conversation about how they are doing, something they have done lately, or a current project they are working on. Keep in mind, grade disputes should not be handled in the hallway and are best left to the email inbox or a visit during office hours. You don't want to offend or bother them by asking a difficult question about a schedule problem or a recent exam grade. If you are someone who knows the limits of polite conversation, then these professors and administrators will remember you.

POWER HOUR - PROFESSOR OFFICE HOURS

Professors are required to be present in their offices for a number of hours each week. View this time as an opportunity for you. The instructors are waiting to give precious time and free advice to any student brave enough to stop by. Unfortunately, the majority of college students never utilize office hours, yet if used properly, they can be some of the most effective time periods of college.

Just like the student who participates in class, the student who visits office hours rises above his peers in his professor's mind. Your strategic and sincere presence demonstrates that you care about your education. In turn, the professor respects you even more, and as mentioned before, being well-regarded by your professors leads to great possibilities like recommendations for special opportunities, as well as scholarships. But most importantly, it's a great opportunity for free advice and insight on a variety of topics.

> *Just like the student who participates in class, the student who visits office hours rises above his peers in his professor's mind.*

VISITING THE SELECTORS

When trying to win a particular scholarship, find out from a past winner what faculty members are responsible for making the selection. Then meet with those faculty in person a few weeks prior to the deadline. Research their involvement with particular programs or departments. If a particular professor is of a higher title, like a tenured member of a department, it is probable he or she will have the selection power you're looking for, or be in touch with the people who do.

Once you find out who these professors are, attend their office hours. It is helpful to create a reason why you need their advice. To do this, research their involvement within their particular field to determine their area of expertise and specialization. Structure the purpose of your visit around their expertise. Ask questions about something that interests you, which they also happen to care about.

Do at least a small amount of background research on the person you are meeting. Usually, if this person is a professor at a distinguished university or a top-level administrator, you can uncover plenty of interesting information about him or her through a Google search or your university's website. This information provides a better understanding of how to connect with the professor or administrator.

After you do your research, create an outline and agenda. Until you develop a solid relationship with your professors and the other administrators with whom you visit, ensure you are well-prepared for the meeting and go in with a purpose. This highlights your organization and focus, and also prevents you from wasting time. When creating your agenda, consider these key discussion points:

- Past work experience (theirs and yours)
- Their motivation to become a professor
- Classes they teach
- Research they are involved with
- If they perform outside consulting work for companies
- Their involvement within the university
- Clubs and organizations they recommend
- Defining characteristics they notice of distinguished students graduating at the top of their class
- Tips on making the most of the college experience
- Community involvement

///////////
Ensure you are well-prepared for the meeting and go in with a purpose.

You should bring something to write on like a legal pad. Several professors and administrators I formed relationships with said they think much more highly of those students who make the effort to write down their advice and key points. The key is not to be a time waster and to go in with a purpose. These faculty will know if you are trying to use them for something when a deadline is approaching, such as a recommendation letter or acceptance into a program, so it is best to build the relationship early.

Office hours are usually posted publicly, but sometimes it is necessary to make an appointment. You may also need to make an appointment if you are attempting to visit a professor whom you have never met and don't have for a class. It is best to do so through an email. Here's an example of an appropriate email you could send:

Professor Slivka,

*I am a freshman studying marketing and entrepreneur-
ship. My friend/advisor (insert your referring person's
name here), recommended I contact you regarding some
marketing issues I'm having involving a business that pays
for my college tuition.*

*I also noticed you have published several books relating
to this topic, as well as worked as a VP of marketing in
the pharmaceutical industry in the past, and I would
appreciate the opportunity to hear about your experiences
and get your advice.*

*Would you mind if I stop by during your office hours? If not,
when would be an optimal time? The best days for me are
Tuesdays and Thursdays from 1-3pm.*

*Thank you for your time,
Brian Smith
bsmith@aniversity.edu*

This email introduces you, builds rapport, conveys the purpose
of the meeting, and provides a few suggested meeting times
from which to choose.

Ensure you arrive at the office on time and dress appropriately
in business casual attire. Greet him or her with a smile and
a handshake and take a seat when one is offered. Open the
conversation by thanking him or her for the time and let the
discussion and your agenda items flow from there.

THE BOOK RECOMMENDATION SECRET

The key to connecting with faculty is learning to see from their perspective. To begin, find out what they like to read. When you visit a professor during office hours, always ask him what some of his favorite books are. Most academic-type people love to read and love to talk with others about what they are reading. One of the easiest ways to connect with a faculty member is to get a recommendation on a book, discuss the book at a later time, and thank him for the recommendation. If the professor recommends a book and you take the time to read it, it gives you a reason to follow up with that person. The professor sees you've trusted the recommendation and received value from it. This interaction builds the relationship between the two of you.

Additionally, ask the professor about her current research, as well as what initiatives and committees she's involved with around campus. Convey your sincere interest and discover how the professor might be able to help you around campus.

Mention your scholarship search sometime over the course of one of your discussions. Convey that you are working very diligently to position yourself as a stand-out candidate. If the professor knows you are looking, she will want to help you and connect you with the right people. For example, if you happen to mention to your finance professor that you have been spending time searching for scholarships, she is likely either to be on a scholarship committee, or know someone on another committee, and could easily put you in contact with the right person. Just like successful students, successful faculty are usually connected with all aspects of the university experience and can point you in the direction toward the richest mine of scholarships.

AARON'S TIP

////////////

THINK LIKE THE FACULTY
Prior to your visits with faculty members, envision yourself in their positions, and consider how you would want students to approach and connect with you. Replay your agenda and visualize yourself talking to the professors to ensure that they will perceive you in a favorable manner.

FOLLOW-UP AND MAINTAIN RELATIONSHIPS

It's best not to go to office hours just once, or whenever you need something. Maintain the relationship through strategic follow-up tactics. Faculty are busy, and while they do enjoy conversing with students, it can become tiresome to see a particular student too frequently. Thus, schedule your meetings strategically. What's more, this is meant to create a real and lasting relationship between you and the professor. It's inappropriate to use faculty for personal gain, and then discard them.

Many of the top students on campus build relationships with faculty members and make an effort to maintain them. While enrolled in a course, these students will visit a professor for the first time usually in the second week of class to avoid the rush and business of the first week. Then, to maintain the relationship. they will drop in, even if only for a few minutes, every few weeks. This periodic one-on-one time keeps the relationship fresh and prevents you from becoming a nuisance. Follow up periodically via email, which professors often prefer after you have finished their classes. A short email exchange once-per-month or so can do wonders for building and maintaining a relationship. Many professors also like to go to lunch with their students, so offer to meet them at one of their favorite restaurants on campus and catch up. Inviting your favorite instructors to lunch can help keep you connected and cultivate the relationship. By staying close with these faculty members, you will continue to remain fresh in their minds and have them as a resource for finding scholarships, and even locating future jobs or internships.

////////////////////////////

HELP PROFESSORS FOR PAY

Many professors have a budget from the university from which they are allowed to employ a few students. Finding these opportunities benefits you in three ways. First, you get paid to do intellectually stimulating work. Second, you form a closer relationship with the professor and others in the department. And third, you learn from someone who is at the top of his or her field. These opportunities are highly selective, and similar to scholarships, you find them by asking around and being known as someone whom the professor would like to work with. When visiting office hours, be sure to mention your interest in these research opportunities.

MAKE MORE CONNECTIONS
WITH INFLUENTIAL PEOPLE

Along with professors and faculty members, there are two other sources that can be extremely influential in helping you maximize your scholarships, and in making connections for the job of your dreams after graduation.

Every school has a board of directors and successful alumni who are more accessible than you think. They are usually very willing to give to the community, as they have likely had a positive experience with the university and want you to do the same. The office of alumni relations manages the information of its graduates, and its job is to keep the alumni connected with the university. This office can provide you with the contact information of people in your future field whom you can contact.

Most of the time, all you need to do is take action, be persistent, and write emails to connect with these people. If you send 10-20 properly written emails, at least a few alumni are bound to respond. In the email introduce yourself, build a connection, and express what it is you want to accomplish, whether it is obtaining an extraordinary job or financing your education through scholarships.

> Alumni will often be more than willing to help you because they remember themselves in the same position years ago, and frequently they will have some good advice for you.

These alumni will often be more than willing to help you because they remember themselves in the same position years ago, and frequently they will have some good advice for you. If you use similar strategies for networking as listed previously, they may even be willing to make a phone call to someone of influence on your behalf. You'd be surprised at what you can achieve just by taking that first step to connect with people. Often all it takes to move up on a scholarship list is a recommendation from a prominent alumnus or professor, so it pays to connect with various alumni and begin to build relationships with them.

AARON'S STORY

I knew a lot of faculty in high school and saw many benefits from these relationships, so I realized the importance, even prior to coming to campus, of building a strong network and having a good reputation. Before and after arriving at school, I worked hard to meet the right people and figure out the best path to success at a large university. I also knew the importance of a strong peer group and made an effort to surround myself with highly ambitious and intelligent friends who helped challenge me.

Early on, I asked the honors program coordinator and advisors to put me in touch with students they knew who had been awarded many scholarships, and they gladly gave me a list of several they thought would be happy to help. Additionally, they provided me with advice on my scholarship search and help in the selection process

I followed up with the students they recommended, had meetings with several of them, and even built friendships with a few. All were happy to share their advice and seemed genuinely excited about the prospect of helping someone else achieve his goals. As a result of their personal experiences and the experiences of their friends, they gave me several recommendations of scholarships to apply to. They also recommended I talk with a few faculty members of the business school who were influential in making the decisions on the awards. Some even offered to help review my applications, essays, and resume and were helpful later on in the interview process by offering me tips and connecting me with professors who were involved with the selection process.

////////////
I worked hard to meet the right people and figure out the best path to success at a large university.

One of the students who had been awarded the entrepreneurship scholarship recommended I talk with a particular entrepreneurship professor in charge of decision making for that scholarship. Prior to the meeting, my friend advised me on the topics about which the professor cared. Based on my friend's suggestions I then crafted a meeting agenda that allowed me to present myself to the professor and build a connection with him, while subtly demonstrating I was the ideal candidate for the scholarship.

I scheduled an appointment with the professor during his office hours and talked with him about my past accomplishments, future ideas, and prospective involvement in the entrepreneurship program. I asked about his vision for the program, and how the students could lead it in that direction. I also told him a few stories about my business experiences and what I had learned from those opportunities. I then related my experiences to my education at school. This is where the small business I ran during college came in handy. It made my interactions with faculty much easier through providing me legitimate topics to discuss and questions to ask, ultimately making me stand out from other students. Through this meeting, the professor recognized my passion for entrepreneurship, and the fact I was someone ideal for the entrepreneurship scholarship.

Always sign up for your department's email list. You can gain valuable information from those simple emails.

I also asked the professor if he had a book that he would recommend I read. He certainly did. I purchased it that night, finished it two weeks later, then emailed him a follow-up about it and thanked him for his recommendation a week before I knew the selection committee was scheduled to meet.

The evening before the committee meeting I happened to receive an email that said the professor would be speaking to a business school club. (Always sign up for your department's email list. You can gain valuable information from those simple emails.) I made a point to attend this meeting and talk with him afterward. These two strategic moves kept me fresh in his mind and made me stand out as a student highly involved within the school's programs.

To my great fortune and as a result of my persistence, a week after the committee met I was notified I had been selected for a scholarship valued at several thousand dollars. I followed the steps above precisely and achieved these results, and you can too. It's just a matter of taking effective and efficient action.

key takeaways
from chapter 6

//////////

1   Attending, paying attention, and
    participating in class will significantly
    improve your reputation among
    professors.

2   Visiting office hours will help you build
    lasting and influential relationships
    with people who are good to know.

3   When you visit office hours, take the
    professors' advice seriously and follow
    up to maintain the relationship.

4   Staying in contact with professors and
    administrators allows them to know
    about your involvement and influence
    in the university community.

5   A strong recommendation from
    a professor is very useful when
    a scholarship requires a recommenda-
    tion letter, but you must build the
    relationship with this person first.

part 3
The Selection Process and Submitting a Winning Application

///////////////////

This section covers the selection process and how to create a winning application with outstanding essays, and recommendation letters.

chapter 7
/////////
Understand the Selection Process

BY UNDERSTANDING THE PROCESS, YOU CAN MAKE IT WORK IN YOUR FAVOR AND BE ON YOUR WAY TO MAXIMIZING YOUR SCHOLARSHIPS.

Some people are better than other people when it comes to Googling. This sounds silly, but it's true. Some people understand exactly the types of words and phrases to enter into a search bar in order to get a desired search result. Other people who think they do an adequate job of Googling, in fact miss out on their actual desired result because they don't really understand how Google works. If you want to use a system, any system, then you must understand how it works in order to get your desired result.

Most students think that the process of selecting scholarship winners is either random or solely dependent on the involvement and GPA of the candidates. This misconception often causes potential winners to give up, without even trying. The selection process isn't that simple; however, by knowing the system you can learn how to position yourself for success, no matter what your GPA is and how involved you are. Once again, it's dependent on who you know and his or her impression of you. This is because a few key people are often in charge of disbursing the majority of a university's or particular department's scholarships. It's usually clear to committees which students understand the process, enabling these students to rise above their peers with greater GPAs and more involvements.

SELECTION CRITERIA EXPLAINED

The criteria committees examine when awarding scholarships depends on a variety of factors. Scholarships are usually funded by donors who dictate the type of candidates the scholarship targets; therefore, it is the job of the committee to ensure that those selected fit the ideal candidate the donor wants. Universities themselves, including specific schools within the university, also fund scholarships, and these go to candidates meeting specific requirements.

Other scholarships are based on financial need, the premise of working your way through school, or campus and community involvement. By understanding the criteria of the scholarship and the intention of the person who endowed it, you can be sure to prepare yourself accordingly and tailor your story to make it more compatible with the requirements. The more background knowledge you have on a particular scholarship, the more prepared you will be. And as always, if you know who to talk to about the scholarship, he or she can help you find your way to success.

////////////
Winning often comes down to your reputation and relationships on campus.

SELECTION PROCESS EXPLAINED

The scholarship selection process primarily depends on the type of scholarship being offered. If it is a larger, very popular scholarship, then the selection process will be a lengthy one. On the other hand, the outcome for some of the smaller scholarships can rest on the judgment of just one or two people. But as you have learned, winning often comes down to your reputation and relationships on campus.

Most commonly, scholarships are awarded based on the decisions of a committee. A few prominent faculty members, the family of the donor, and some advisors and administrators comprise the typical committee. The key is to find out who these people are and then get on their radar. Discover what matters to them in making their selection (e.g. reputation, campus involvement, future plans, etc).

These committee members are often people who have a presence in the campus community, and you can usually find out their identity by asking around, particularly by asking students who have won in the past. These students have had many interactions with the committee members during their application process and can guide you as to the issues and ideas important to each committee member.

For example, an entrepreneurship professor would think more highly of a student if she knew the student was running his own business, as well as was involved in the young entrepreneurs association at the school.

THINK LIKE THE COMMITTEE

Depending on the scholarship, you may need to write several essays, which obviously get read by someone. But imagine what the review committee members feel when they have a stack of a few hundred essays to read in order to make a decision.

Many times the committee members either take the essays home over a weekend to read through and flag the favorites, or they divide and conquer. In this instance, each member reads a set of essays, picks a favorite or two, and then reconvenes to discuss the findings.

See **Chapter 4** for tips on writing your story in a compelling way.

Why is this knowledge important? Because while writing your essays, you must think of the person who ultimately reviews them. Therefore, don't exceed the word limits or have any grammatical or spelling errors in your submission. You must also write in a compelling way to make your story unique, as covered in Chapter 4.

ELIMINATION ROUND

When the committee reconvenes, they will deliberate over the quality of the essays and will share the top ones among the members. Once your application and essay make it past the elimination round, your reputation comes into play.

The members will discuss what they personally know of the candidate, along with the quality of his or her essay. Issues on the table for discussion include academic success, university involvement and contribution, interactions among peers, as well as the candidate's future potential.

At this point, who you know and who knows you is very important because people on the committee can speak on your behalf, which could lead to your selection as the winner.

GET NOTICED

After spending years serving on scholarship committees and reading endless essays, faculty are able to easily decipher the level of passion and motivation of the candidates through their writing style and quality. An essay, application, or interview backed with passion stands out above the others because true emotion shines through the writing. Such an essay clearly conveys the student's desire to win and his or her will to succeed. Committee members often read many outstanding essays because the students applying for these scholarships are generally good writers; however, when they come across an essay telling an interesting story and creatively addressing the prompt, it stands out. The key to rising to the top of a massive stack of essays is to help the committee members share your excitement. Make the reviewers excited, and they are likely to select your essay for discussion in the scholarship meeting.

An essay, application, or interview backed with passion stands out above the others because true emotion shines through the writing.

RISE TO THE TOP AND BE MEMORABLE

There are several key points of differentiation between the winners and losers of scholarships. The selection process is often such a lengthy one the committees are forced to create certain criteria that allow them immediately to throw out an application. This enables the group to focus solely on the well-written essays. Here are some of the common criteria committees use.

Does your application look nice?

The first criterion is simple. Does your application look nice? If you are required to submit the application in paper form, be sure to use a high quality resume paper. You can buy 100 sheets of this paper for $10 at your local office supply store. You don't want all of your hard work and accomplishments put on library printer paper, so be sure to show some pride in your work and present your case on quality paper. Your application will stand out, and that's exactly what you want it to do.

Is your application accurate?

Next, the selection committee will consider the accuracy of your application. Turning in an application with errors is a poor reflection of your character and work ethic. If you don't care enough to spend the time checking your work, then the committee shouldn't care enough to spend the time reading it. Have multiple friends proofread your application, but be sure to choose friends who are strong writers. Don't simply choose your roommate because he or she happens to be in the room. Even something as small as forgetting your phone number on a page or spelling your city wrong can cost you the scholarship. It's not worth the risk. Take your time, and proofread your work several times.

> You don't want all of your hard work and accomplishments put on library printer paper, so be sure to show some pride in your work and present your case on quality paper.

Do you have a respectable GPA?

The committee will also check to see if you have a respectable GPA. A low grade point average reflects poorly on your character. As previously stated, many of the committee members are also professors, and if you have a mediocre grade point average, it communicates you don't care about what they are passionate about–education. No matter your innate ability or outside involvements, your goal should be to maintain a 3.0 GPA. This number is often the cut-off for many scholarships because a GPA below this threshold often communicates an indifference toward your studies. A highly competitive GPA is 3.5 or above. Don't worry if you don't have a 4.0 because the rest of the committee's decision depends on other qualitative factors such as your character, reputation, and involvement.

///////////
No matter your innate ability or outside involvements, your goal should be to maintain a 3.0 GPA.

Are you a familiar name and face around the school?

If you've been able to stay in the competition based on the above factors, then less measurable factors come into play. Has the committee ever heard your name on campus? The majority of scholarship winners tend to have strong reputations within their specific schools or departments. Name recognition really isn't difficult and comes as a result of spending time getting to know professors and administrators, such as advisors and the school's program and admission coordinators.

Are you well-rounded?

Another consideration is whether you demonstrate commitment to something else along with your education. Committees want to see students who are well-rounded members of a community. Surprisingly, students with a 4.0 GPA often will be tossed aside because they don't demonstrate a passion for something outside of their studies. Therefore, have a hobby or another commitment such as playing an intramural sport or being highly involved with something you enjoy like volunteering, training for a marathon, or running a side business.

Are you deserving?

Are you deserving of the scholarship? Scholarships buy you some degree of freedom on campus, and if you obtain several of them, you may get to the point where you won't need to hold a job during the school year. The committee must have the confidence you will utilize this freedom productively, rather than socializing at the bars or playing video games all the time. If you can clarify how you will use this freedom, either through your essay or personal interactions with the committee, they will be much more likely to select you.

The committee will also consider how you will use the money. If you have a lot of money and flaunt it openly, the committee will be less likely to award you the scholarship because there is probably another student who needs it more than you do. Therefore, it is important to always act modestly.

If you have a lot of money and flaunt it openly, the committee will be less likely to award you the scholarship because there is probably another student who needs it more than you do.

Will you be a good face for the program?

Universities love featuring scholarship winners prominently on their websites, as well as in some newspapers and other publications. Various individuals will see these winners, such as prospective students and others who will use the winners' characters to make a judgment on the school as a whole. If you convey you will be an honorable scholar and a great ambassador for the school, you are more likely to be chosen.

////////
You need to transmit confidence without coming off as conceited.

Are you an individual?

Successful people are not afraid to do their own thing. They are different, and it shows, whether it be through their writing style, their attitude, or their pride. Being confident in your future success is apparent to others, even through the application and selection process, but you need to transmit confidence without coming off as conceited. The committee wants to see you are your own person. If you display this proper attitude, you will likely rise to the top.

WINNING TAKES STRATEGY

The selection process comes down to thinking like the committee and considering what they look for in a candidate. Once you have an understanding of how they go about making their decision, you will have a better idea of how to optimally present yourself to them.

key takeaways
from chapter 7

/////////////////

1   The better you understand the selection process, the more likely you are to be selected.

2   Think like the committee and ensure you appeal to them.

3   Differentiate yourself and avoid the commonly made mistakes that will get your application tossed.

4   Build your reputation in the school, especially among the selection committee members, and work to get to know them.

chapter 8

Write a Winning Application

A PROPERLY WRITTEN APPLICATION WILL ELEVATE YOUR NAME TO THE TOP OF A LIST OF POTENTIAL CANDIDATES.

Why don't you sound the same as your favorite musician when you sing your favorite song in the shower? It's the same song. It's the same words. So why would an audience react so negatively if they were to hear your version? It's simple. It's all about delivery. The same song, sung by the right person, will always sound better. If you view your scholarship application in this way, then you will be the person who sings the right song.

So how can you separate yourself through a standardized application process? There are several ways, and by following these strategies, you will be certain to rise to the top of the applicant pool. The application process consists of several components which allow the committee to make a judgment on your character and to get an idea of who you really are and what you are capable of. If you pass the test and get their attention, you can position yourself for the win.

////////////////////

Depending on the scholarship, the process may include a general application form with informational questions, short answer questions, essays, a resume requirement, and an interview with the committee, if you happen to be selected for the final round.

Many books focus just on the application process. However, this book gives you a holistic view of everything required in making yourself an optimal candidate for scholarships. Simply applying for random scholarships without following the other steps is like building a house without a foundation. It will fall down, just like your application will fall out of the running for being selected if you don't lay the groundwork by developing your network, creating your story, and establishing a pristine reputation.

When you combine a solid application, which we will show you how to write, with a unique approach strategy, a solid network, and an impeccable campus reputation, you will be an optimal candidate and well on your way to maximizing your scholarships.

STEP 1: KNOW WHAT YOU'RE APPLYING FOR

The first step in applying to win is making yourself knowledgeable of what you're applying for. You won't win the scholarship if you don't know the purpose or details behind it. For example, many donors who endow scholarships establish them based on certain criteria or for students fitting a specific mold. It is the selection committee's job to use their best judgment to ensure they choose the right candidates.

Set yourself apart by knowing the details of the scholarship and information about the person who established it. If the scholarship you're applying for was endowed by a successful scientist or top executive, it's to your benefit to develop background knowledge on his or her career. Often the committee makes their selection based on the potential within a candidate, and if you learn about the lives and careers of the scholarship founders, you portray ambition and stand out in the eyes of the committee.

It also is to your benefit not only to know about the background of the person establishing the scholarship, but also to know the purpose of the scholarship. Maybe it is to help working students pay their way through school. If so, you would want to communicate how you're working through school, how that experience benefits you, and how you appreciate your education more so because of it.

AARON'S TIP
///////////
By knowing the requirements and background of the scholarship well, you will be ahead of many others who blindly apply. It puts you ahead of the game because you have an idea of what the committee wants, and therefore will be able to connect with them better.

You are not alone if you are wondering, "Where do I find this information?" Fortunately, there is an easy answer to this question. Use the Internet! Often scholarships are identified by the names of the donors, so all you need to do is perform a Google search of the name of the scholarship + your university. This search should uncover plenty of valuable information. In addition, find out in what field the donor was involved by searching his name + his field on the Internet. For example, if a scholarship was endowed by John Galt, an entrepreneur in the transportation industry, you can search "John Galt+rail lines" on Google and you will be sure to locate the information you are looking for.

When reading through this information, take down some key notes about how the donor lived his life and try to uncover his guiding principles so you can model your essay accordingly. Guiding principles are the essence of a person. Is he charitable? Is he a self-made success? Learn about his life, and understand what sort of applicant he would appreciate.

In an interview situation, the committee is certain to ask a question regarding the scholarship's purpose or history, so it will distinguish you from the other candidates if you can answer this question intelligently. For example, the committee might ask, "What was Mr. Galt's purpose when he established this scholarship and what type of students did he want to help?"

If you speak intelligently about the scholarship and its founder, you establish yourself as a well-prepared, passionate and respectful individual because you took the time to investigate the background information. Follow this step and not only will you be more prepared and able to write a better essay, but also you will validate yourself as a great potential candidate.

////////////

If you speak intelligently about the scholarship and its founder, you establish yourself as a well-prepared, passionate and respectful individual because you took the time to investigate the background information.

STEP 2: INITIATE CONTACT

Get on the committee's radar prior their review of the applications and essays. You can accomplish this goal through networking with the faculty, as discussed earlier, but also through initiating strategic contact. Here are three popular methods to do so.

1. *Email or call the scholarship administrator or someone on the committee to introduce yourself and ask an intelligent question regarding the scholarship.*
2. *Visit this person briefly in his or her office when you pick up the application.*
3. *Include an introductory letter or cover letter with your application.*

When you complete one or all of the above, you make the administrator look forward to your application. You spark curiosity about you, and the curiosity of the committee is your path to the top of the stack of applications. If you stimulate the committee's interest in you by initiating contact prior to the review, as well as by telling them a unique story, you increase your chances of an interview, as well as focus their attention while they review your application.

HOW TO WRITE THE INITIAL EMAIL

For some of the larger scholarships, an administrator coordinates the program, and when you introduce yourself through an email or phone call, you've opened your relationship with him or her in a positive way. Use the background knowledge you acquired on the scholarship to intelligently develop your question and relate it to your background. Ask a question about the traits of the previous winners. Show you are highly interested in the scholarship and want to set yourself apart from the crowd.

The key is to build an introductory email around your question. Below is an example of an effective introductory email.

EMAIL TEXT

Mrs. Rand,

My name is Brian Smith and I am a freshman studying sports marketing. I found out about this scholarship through my consumer marketing professor, Jeremy Epps, and he strongly encouraged me to apply.

The background of the donor is very interesting to me and I aspire to follow a similar path with my career. My hope is to one day give back to my alma mater after achieving great success, as he has.

I know this is a very popular scholarship, and I was wondering what the key characteristics were that you recognized in your past winners. What did these winners do to stand out to you and your committee during the selection process?

This scholarship is very important to me and would allow me to do a great deal with my time on campus. I want to turn in the best application possible.

I look forward to your reply. Thank you for your time, and I hope for the opportunity to meet with you for an interview.

Sincerely,

Brian Smith
bsmith@auniversity.edu

The committee will notice an email like this one for several reasons. At the same time, a response to the email will answer your questions and give you some tips on what to do to further differentiate yourself.

The email begins with an introduction and a mention of a faculty member. This communicates your relationship with a distinguished professor and his or her recommendation of you, which in turn links you with that professor in the administrator's mind. Next, the email reveals you have done your background research and are familiar with the donor and the scholarship. Additionally, it mentions your admiration for the donor, his or her contribution to the university, and your plan to follow suit after achieving great success. This conveys your ambition and your value as a future alumnus.

////////// Your email alone will set you apart from most applicants.

Next, the question you pose in the email not only gives a reason for the email, but also allows you to unearth some ideal traits in previously selected winners. Your email communicates the importance of the scholarship to you, and it mentions that it will allow you make an impact on campus. Thus, you prove you value your education and want to make a contribution to the university.

Finally, conclude by thanking the administrator for his or her time to read your email and write a response. Indicate you hope for the opportunity to discuss your application in person or with committee in the future.

This initial email alone will set you apart from most applicants. Can you believe how easy that was? Yet, so many students blindly turn in their applications without further thought. It's like applying for a job without first initiating contact and trying to build a relationship with the recruiters. Your job application would be tossed out. But by using the above strategy, you create expectancy among the committee and they will look forward to hearing your story.

MAKE THE PHONE CALL

Instead of an email, another option is to make a phone call to the scholarship coordinator or person in charge of answering questions. An ideal phone call would follow the context of the previous email. Ensure you are prepared prior to calling, then make the call and speak with a confident voice.

Refer to the scholarship and who recommended you apply and why. Then follow the previous steps for the ideal email and ask your question. Be sure to thank the person, and you can even follow up the call with a thank-you email.

The key is initiating contact in any way possible, but there is a fine line between being effective and being annoying. If you appear insincere, ask foolish questions, or waste this person's time, he or she will become resentful, and it will reflect poorly in your review process.

INCLUDE A COVER LETTER

The number one action that instantly sets your application apart is the inclusion of a cover letter explaining your situation and relating it to the scholarship. Almost no scholarship will require a cover letter, but the fact you included one will immediately differentiate your application and allow you to highlight the specific reasons you should be selected. As the committee reads it, you ignite curiosity about you because rarely will any other applicant include a letter.

The ideal cover letter is efficient and effective in that it is short, yet conveys a very powerful message with its words.

KEYS TO A WINNING COVER LETTER

1. *Address the letter to the scholarship selection committee.*
2. *Thank them for the opportunity to apply and for their time to read your application.*
3. *Tell them something unique about yourself and relate it to the scholarship.*
4. *Describe how the scholarship would allow you to be more involved on campus.*
5. *Highlight your commitment to the university and to yourself and others.*
6. *Tell them how the scholarship would help you achieve your goals.*
7. *Thank them again.*
8. *Add that you would appreciate the opportunity for an interview to further discuss your ambitions, and to answer their questions.*

Next is an example of a letter that won several thousand in scholarships, and if you submit something similar to this along with your application, you will be well on your way to winning.

LETTER TEXT

Brian Smith
1250 N. Jordan Ave.
West Lafayette, IN 48940

A University Foundation
Scholarship Selection Committee
5142 Jackson St.
Oxford, OH 45056

September 23, 2008

Dear Sally Hall and the Scholarship Selection Committee:

Thank you for reviewing my application and I appreciate the opportunity to apply for this generous scholarship. I am working to pay my own way through school as a result of several entrepreneurial ventures, and I have been successful to this point. I made this agreement with my parents upon graduating high school because I knew I would place more value in my degree if I were the one responsible for paying for it. A scholarship like this one would be very helpful because it would allow me to spend more time focusing on my studies and getting involved in university activities rather than spending my spare time working.

I value and respect this school, and after being accepted, I have done my best to get involved and become a productive member of the student body. I understand the many benefits of being involved on campus and building my network, and I am working to make the most of my opportunity here to create a strong foundation for my future.

I am actively involved as the president of my pledge class for my fraternity and also in the orientation events and mentor program for incoming students. In addition, I have strong entrepreneurial interests and operate a small business that has provided me with many opportunities to apply what I learn in the classroom to the business world.

This scholarship would allow me to continue funding my college education on my own terms. I also understand the value of giving back to the university, and in the future I plan on contributing to the foundation in order to help young students, like myself, achieve their goals. Thank you again for your time in reading my essays and reviewing my application. I look forward to meeting you for an interview and answering any questions you may have.

Sincerely,
Brian F. Smith
bsmith@auniversity.edu

////////////

If you include a cover letter like this you immediately set a favorable tone for your application and almost guarantee advancement to a subsequent round, provided the remaining parts of your application are strong.

SUBMIT A WINNING APPLICATION

All of your hard work locating the scholarships, contacting the winners, meeting the committee, and writing a great cover letter can be absolutely wasted if you turn in a weak application. Avoiding student loans is hard work that requires a great strategy. Understanding how to write the perfect application is an important part to that strategy.

There are various types of applications, depending upon the scholarship and the collection system. Some will be online and use a form, while others will require you to print them and fill in. The key here is to ensure the application is accurate and fully complete.

> Typing your application not only makes it easier for the committee to read but also makes you appear more organized.

If you use a paper copy, be sure to print it on quality paper, as discussed in the selection process chapter, as this will help get it noticed. Even if the application is a form you print and hand-write, you can stand out if you find a way to type it. This makes it look neater if perhaps you have the same handwriting you had in third grade.

Typing your application not only makes it easier for the committee to read but also makes you appear more organized. It is another variable that sets you apart. If the application is submitted online, precede it with an email or letter to the person receiving it. This is another great touch.

WRITE A WINNING ESSAY: BE THE BEST YOU

The scholarship essays allow the committee to get a clear picture of each candidate. You communicate your personality, or lack thereof, through your writing ability. The good news, however, is you can learn how to write a good essay, an essay that will get you through to the next round of interviews.

Too often students rush the writing process and therefore produce a poorly written essay. Essays are part of the process for a reason: the committee weeds out the undeserving candidates.

The better your writing ability, the more intelligent you sound. However, you don't need to be an incredible writer to construct a winning essay. The first thing you need to do is learn these three steps for writing an effective scholarship application essay.

THE KEYS TO A WINNING ESSAY

1.   *Creatively address the question*
2.   *Organize the essay in a logical structure*
3.   *Share something unique about yourself*

When the committee reads hundreds of essays in a short period of time, the essays blend together, except the few done in a creative fashion.

TIME SAVING SECRET

The great thing about a quality essay is once you write a few of them, you can reuse the majority of their components. There are only a few types of prompts, and if you apply for enough scholarships, you will have saved an essay addressing the basic features of each variety of prompt. All you need to do is update the essay slightly and modify it to reflect the difference in the scholarship, as well as anything you have accomplished since it was originally written. This saves you time and makes you more likely to apply for more scholarships.

People naturally resist tasks when they think it requires a large amount of initial work. However, you break this psychological barrier when you have already completed essays. Think about it. It might take you five hours initially to write a wonderful essay, but once you have written it, you will only need to spend about an hour or so revising it each time you submit it for something new.

AARON'S TIP

It might take you five hours initially to write a wonderful essay, but once you have written it, you will only need to spend about an hour or so revising it each time you submit it for something new.

WHY MOST STUDENTS DON'T APPLY FOR SCHOLARSHIPS

The main reason most of your classmates won't apply for scholarships is the essay requirement, and if you break through this barrier a few times, you will acquire a toolbox of essays to reuse in the future. The essay is the gatekeeper for scholarships and one of its jobs is to reduce the number of applicants. For most students, writing essays for scholarships is overwhelming because of all the writing they already do for their classes. But it's important to see the long term benefits.

> The essay is the gatekeeper for scholarships, and one of its jobs is to reduce the number of applicants.

PREPARE FOR A GOOD ESSAY

The foundation for a winning essay comes well before you even learn of the scholarship. It starts with what you do in your free time, and the activities with which you choose to be involved. The more experiences you have, the better story you will be able to tell the committee.

WRITE TO THE PROMPT

When writing your essay, you first must fully understand the question or prompt. The committee will look to a few specific criteria when reviewing your essay, and one of the first is whether or not you understand and address the main points of the prompt. Therefore, be sure to read and reread your essay to make sure you actually address the prompt.

FOLLOW A LOGICAL STRUCTURE

After the content, the structure is the most important part of your essay. If you have great content but it doesn't flow logically, then you can't communicate your message and story to the committee.

In the introduction, begin by directly addressing the prompt and developing a thesis statement based off of the prompt and your personal experiences. Then use the body of the essay to tell a story and relate your experiences to the prompt.

For example, if the prompt states, "Describe your most gratifying entrepreneurial experience," you want to begin with something such as, "My most gratifying entrepreneurial experience thus far has been seeing how the lessons I learn in the classroom apply to the business world through my creation of several small businesses." Then follow up with a thesis statement such as, "Although some of my businesses have been successful, and others have failed, each experience has continuously challenged me as an entrepreneur."

Capture the attention of the readers and ignite the spark of their curiosity from the beginning of your essay. These initial two sentences do just that. First, the sentences address the prompt, and then they distinguish you as an entrepreneur. In addition, they demonstrate the value you place on your experiences and education. By capturing the committee's attention, you make them want to reader further, rather than tossing your writing aside. Many committee members admit they "move on" if they are not intrigued after reading the first paragraph or two of an essay.

Next, recount a story highlighting your experiences. It should relate to your thesis and describe the lessons you learned through your experiences. Spotlight your ambitions and your drive to succeed through a story about your perserverence through adversity.

> *Capture the attention of the readers and ignite the spark of their curiosity from the beginning of your essay.*

Remember, a well written essay enables you to stand out among the other applicants and clearly showcases your drive to succeed. Be sure to follow the steps to creatively address the prompt, build a thesis statement, and then tell a unique story that supports the thesis.

BUILD A CONCLUSION

The conclusion is another critical part of your essay. It unifies everything you've written and closes the interaction between your words and the reader. A solid conclusion can make or break the entire essay. The best way to conclude is to restate the thesis through different wording, and then wrap up with a few sentences that gradually usher the readers out of the paper and leave them thinking. For example, your final few sentences could summarize what you have learned, how it has been beneficial to you, and how this experience will contribute to your future success. This type of conclusion leaves the reader with a positive last impression of your ability and potential for future success.

///////////
A solid conclusion can make or break the entire essay.

TYPES OF ESSAYS

Some applications limit the word count of your essay. You need to stay within this limit because the committee often judges you on your ability to follow the instructions of the prompt. Furthermore, the committee wants to see how well you can clearly and concisely construct your thoughts. Some larger scholarships have multiple prompts and allow you to write without limit, but it is best to keep it short and sweet while telling a great story.

KEY CONCEPTS TO EMPHASIZE IN YOUR ESSAY

Including a few key concepts in your essay strikes a connection with the readers and causes your essay to stand out among the pack. One great strategy is to describe your respect for the scholarship donor's career and contribution to the university. Emphasize the fact you value the importance of contributing to the university and its students after you graduate. Your research about the donor is key here. You need to know what you are talking about.

////////
One great essay strategy is to describe your respect for the scholarship donor's career and contribution to the university.

This part of the essay relays important information to the committee. First, it expresses your genuine gratitude and your admiration of achievement. Second, it reveals your ambition and aspiration for great success. Finally, it demonstrates your generosity by acknowledging you value giving back to the community and helping others achieve their dreams.

COMMON PROMPTS

1. Describe your most valuable learning experience and how it has contributed to your success.
2. Who has been most influential to you and what has he or she done to have an impact on your life?
3. Describe your future career plans.
4. Discuss why you would be a worthy recipient of this award.
5. Explain what motivates you and why.
6. What interests you about your chosen field of study?

FINALIZE AND SUBMIT YOUR ESSAY AND APPLICATION

You wouldn't want work this hard on your application only to have an error or two get it thrown out. When you write, it's easy to become absorbed in your ideas and essay structure and miss the flaws in your own writing. Therefore, it's critical to write the essay early enough so that you have time to put it aside for a day or two, and then return to it to revise. Next, have a person with excellent writing ability review it for you. This person will catch errors hidden to you. Our organizational and grammatical errors are often camouflaged to our own eyes; however, they can be very obvious to another reader. A good person to review your essay is a faculty member you are close with or a past winner of the scholarship who you have added to your network and who has given you advice on the process. Most would be happy to help you out. All you have to do is ask. This small step ensures your work doesn't go to waste because of a simple mistake you should have caught.

Once you are finished, turn in your application and essay in a personalized manner. Hand deliver it directly to the coordinator or someone on the committee responsible for collecting the applications. Be sure to get it in early and don't wait until the last minute. Dress appropriately and go directly to the coordinator's office to proudly present your application in person. You attach a face to your name and application and show you care enough about the scholarship to be absolutely certain the committee receives your application. Following these steps will make a lasting impression on the committee and the administrator. But most importantly, it's another part of doing everything possible to make yourself stand out and take an active role in the selection process.

If you are unable to turn in the application in-person, send a short email to the person responsible for collecting it to confirm he or she received your materials. This email puts your name in front of the committee one more time and demonstrates you truly care about turning in your hard work.

OTHER CRITICAL COMPONENTS
///////////
Along with the cover letter and essays, your resume is another important component of the application. Your resume paints a picture of what you do in your spare time and how you focus your efforts. It can be a key piece to stand out from the other candidates. There is more information on creating a great resume at *AvoidStudent Loans.com.*

key takeaways
from chapter 8

//////////////////

1 Be knowledgeable of the scholarship you are applying for and do your background research.

2 Initiate contact with the scholarship administrator or selection committee prior to turning in your application.

3 Turn in your application with a cover letter, whether one is required or not.

4 Reuse your past essays to apply for several scholarships by making only a few light modifications.

5 Emphasize the value of your education and giving back to others in your essays and interactions.

chapter 9
///////

Maximize the Quality and Impact of Recommendation Letters

AN EXCELLENT RECOMMENDATION LETTER REINFORCES WHAT YOU SAY ABOUT YOURSELF IN YOUR ESSAYS AND RESUME BY PROVIDING A THIRD-PARTY PERSPECTIVE. ////////////////

The unfortunate reality is the scholarship process often starts to feel a bit uncomfortable. Why? Because it becomes so self-involved. Frankly, your goal is to prove to a group of people how awesome you are. That, in itself, is kind of strange. Acknowledge this fact and move on. Your ability to tell your story without coming off as pompous is an important lifelong skill. You will use it when winning scholarships, getting your first job, and then maybe someday asking investors to invest millions of dollars in your company.

While learning how to graciously talk about yourself is an important skill to get comfortable with, getting others to eloquently sing your praises is equally important.

The final piece to the scholarship puzzle is obtaining a great recommendation letter from an impressive third party.

Some scholarships may require a recommendation letter along with your other application materials. This serves two purposes. First, it adds another barrier to the scholarship application process in order to filter out applicants who aren't as motivated. Second, it allows the committee to understand the perspective of someone with whom you have formed a close working relationship. Through this person's perspective the committee can gain a more personalized understanding of your personality type, intelligence, and level of ambition.

The right recommendation letter can reinforce your other solid application materials and add another level of distinction to your persona. Not surprisingly, not all recommendation letters are created equally, but the process of obtaining a good one is much more important and controllable than you may think. Just like all the other areas of the scholarship process, there is an actual strategy to maximizing the impact of a recommendation letter, and if followed, it will lead to maximizing your scholarships.

> *There is an actual strategy to maximizing the impact of a recommendation letter, and if followed, it will lead to maximizing your scholarships.*

THREE MAJOR RECOMMENDATION LETTER MISTAKES

There are three major mistakes students make when seeking a recommendation letter for a scholarship:

1. *They don't build a strong relationship with the recommendation writer first.*
2. *They fail to give any guidance on writing the letter.*
3. *They don't review the letter with the writer prior to submission.*

When you commit any of these mistakes, you fail to maximize the impact of your letter and can potentially sacrifice its quality and effect on the committee. Follow the advice below and you will learn the steps to maximize the quality and impact of recommendation letters.

FIND THE RIGHT
RECOMMENDATION WRITER

The first step to obtain an outstanding recommendation letter is to find the right person to write it for you. This individual should have great things to say about you, as well as have influence with the committee. Thus, practice networking, as previously highlighted, to build these key relationships early. The longer you have known the person, the more comfortable he or she will feel in recommending you. By following the steps of proper networking, you build a diverse and powerful network that will provide you with many options when you need someone to write a letter.

AARON'S TIP

When looking for someone to write your letter, it's best to avoid a professor whom you know other students will ask, unless you can be confident he will write a better letter for you than for everyone else. Many students will often ask a popular professor to write recommendation letters, and this can put the professor in a difficult position. If he thinks equally of all the students, he won't have many unique things to say to make you stand out among your peers. Also, some professors use templates or reuse past recommendation letters. This can be detrimental because the letter won't be personalized, so always review the letter with the writer prior to submission.

Ideally, you want your letter writer to be someone who knows you well, is influential in his or her respective field or community, and can effectively communicate these ideas on paper. You don't always need to choose a professor, and in fact, sometimes it's best if you don't. Selecting someone other than a professor shows you have strong outside involvement with powerful people who are willing to write you a glowing recommendation letter. Below are some groups of people to approach when you need a recommendation letter.

Selecting someone other than a professor shows you have strong outside involvement with powerful people who are willing to write you a glowing letter of recommendation.

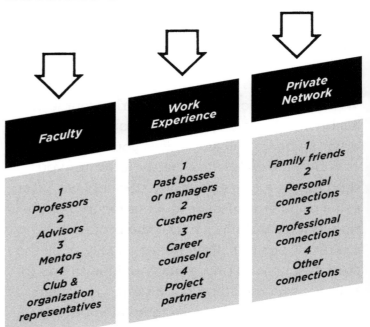

Faculty
1 Professors
2 Advisors
3 Mentors
4 Club & organization representatives

Work Experience
1 Past bosses or managers
2 Customers
3 Career counselor
4 Project partners

Private Network
1 Family friends
2 Personal connections
3 Professional connections
4 Other connections

As you learned earlier, it is important to think like a committee member. Analyze from where you think the ideal recommendation would come for this scholarship. For example, if the scholarship involves entrepreneurship, a recommendation letter from one of your customers would be fitting and valuable. Consider the clout of the individual who will be writing the letter as well. If you do choose a professor, make sure he or she is both well-known and well-respected within your school and around the university. Find a professor who could potentially have friendships with other faculty on the committee. In addition, if you have a strong relationship with someone important from your community, such as a prominent doctor, lawyer, or business owner, it is often beneficial to have him or her write you a letter. The more highly regarded the writer is, the more effective the letter will be. Make the recommendation letter work in your favor by choosing your writer carefully.

ALL YOU HAVE TO DO IS ASK

Many students avoid scholarships requiring a recommendation letter because they don't want to ask someone to take the time to write one for them. What most people don't realize, though, is that others are often flattered when you consider them worthy of writing a recommendation. They were once in your position too and had to go through the same process of obtaining countless recommendation letters. They will expect nothing in return but your gratitude, and they too will share in the excitement if you are to win. The best repayment you can give these individuals is to ensure you put your best effort into the entire scholarship process and win the scholarship.

GUIDE THE LETTER CREATION PROCESS

Your recommendation writers will be even more willing to help if you give them some direction in the process. They are often not familiar with the particular scholarship you are applying for, so provide them with a summary of its background and criteria for selection. And be sure to clarify the details and purpose of the scholarship.

Talk with someone on the committee or in charge of the scholarship to determine the ideal candidate. Then relate the main qualities of this ideal candidate to your recommendation writer. The key is learning what would flatter the committee and getting the writer to put that information into the letter about you. Obtain this information through networking with previous winners and the scholarship administrator.

Identify three to five main personal characteristics you want to convey to the committee. Make sure that your writer also recognizes these qualities within you and can easily highlight them in the letter. Provide a list of activities that showcase your key qualities so that your writer will be able to mention them on your behalf. In essence, you need to write a framework of the letter for him or her. This makes the letter easier to write and leads to a better end product. Providing a starting point also reduces potential procrastination on the writer's part.

For example, if you want your letter writer to highlight your ambition, give her an example, such as how you applied for a grant to study trends in business to develop your knowledge of emerging practices you hope to capitalize on in the future. An example like the one above enables the committee to see others in the community recognize your positive qualities and would certainly make you stand out during the discussion and selection process.

Communicate to the writer why you are applying for the scholarship and what winning would mean to you. If the writer understands the scholarship's level of importance to you, he or she will feel more inspired to help you, and therefore produce a better letter.

GUIDANCE EMAIL EXAMPLE

The best way to direct your recommendation writer is through a friendly, instructional email or letter.

EMAIL TEXT

Dr. Bailey,

I am working on my application for the McCarthy Scholarship at my university and one of the requirements is a recommendation letter from someone who can speak on behalf of my abilities, ambition, and personality.

I am grateful for the relationship we have developed over the past few years and all of the advice you have given me. I think you would be the perfect person to write the required recommendation letter. I'm confident the committee would receive it very favorably.

The scholarship is a $15,000 annual award given to 10 different students who are working to pay their way through school and maximizing their educational opportunities. You can learn more about the scholarship by going to www.McCarthyScholarshipLink.com. I would be extremely grateful for this award because it would allow me to spend less time working hourly to pay for my tuition and more time studying and making the most of all there is to do on campus.

The three key qualities I would like to emphasize to the scholarship committee are my professionalism, my drive to succeed, and my entrepreneurial experience. In order to recognize my professionalism you could reference our interactions and your first impression of me. To highlight my drive to succeed, please mention my diligence in applying what I learn in the classroom to my business ventures. And finally, to accentuate my entrepreneurial ability, you could reference your experience as a customer of my business. Please feel free to include anything else you feel is relevant.

I know you will be able to write me an outstanding letter. Could we meet in two weeks for a review, as the deadline is at the end of the month and I want to get my application in early?

Thank you very much for your time and I really appreciate your help.

Sincerely,
Brian Smith
bsmith@AUniversity.com

////////////

This email is the ideal "ask letter." It clearly identifies its purpose and strengthens the connection between the student and the other party. Then it describes the award and what it would mean to the student to win it. After that, it includes a few ideas the student would like mentioned and examples to include. To conclude, it uses an action request and a thank you.

REVIEW YOUR LETTER

AARON'S TIP
After you have the recommendation letter written, spend time reviewing it with the person who created it. Don't be afraid to ask him or her for a draft and to make a revision. It is better to catch a mistake early and spend a small amount of time revising it than to have the letter go to the committee only to get thrown out because of an error. One time, I received a recommendation letter with the wrong name on it. It was an honest mistake because the professor used the same format template for all his letters. However, it would have looked unprofessional had I submitted that letter to the committee, and it could have potentially cost me the scholarship.

Maximize the Quality and Impact of Recommendation Letters

Often scholarships require recommendation letters to be submitted in a sealed envelope, so once you and your writer discuss the final letter, have him or her put it in an envelope and sign the seal. Therefore, the committee will have absolute confidence you didn't create a recommendation letter for yourself.

Whether required or not, recommendation letters are extremely effective in helping you win scholarships. They provide a third-party perspective of your character and allow the reviewing committee to understand how other important individuals perceive you. They are a critical part of the scholarship selection process. From choosing the right people to recommend you to giving them guidance on how to write the letter, it is important to follow a strategy when obtaining them. A great recommendation letter can be the difference between being selected and receiving a "We're sorry letter." Take this part of the process seriously.

////////////
Whether required or not, recommendation letters are extremely effective in helping you win scholarships.

key takeaways
from chapter 9

1 You must build your relationships with potential recommendation writers early, before you need their letters.

2 Writers can be a variety of people, from your professors to your previous employers.

3 Ask and usually people are happy to write recommendation letters because it makes them feel important.

4 Provide your writers with guidance for the content of the letter so they will highlight key aspects of your character and accomplishments.

5 Review your letters with the writers to ensure they reflect your character and satisfy the requirements of the scholarship.

chapter 10

Leverage
Your
Success

YOU CAN TURN ONE WIN INTO MANY, AS WELL AS CONTINUE YOUR SUCCESS INTO OTHER IMPORTANT AREAS OF YOUR COLLEGE EXPERIENCE AND CAREER, IF YOU MANAGE YOUR WIN PROPERLY.

So you've done it. You've followed the steps in this book, taken action, and ultimately your hard work paid off and you won a scholarship, or hopefully several. Now what you need to do, besides telling your friends about how this book helped you *Avoid Student Loans*, is to ensure you leverage your success. Your behavior after being selected is a determining factor in many matters, from whether you will be chosen for more scholarships in the future to what types of jobs you will be offered upon graduation.

Winning particular scholarships puts you into a select group of people and earns you respect that you should use to your advantage. Once you have been selected by a committee as a winner, you now have a certain level of social credibility which you should put to work. For instance, this newfound credibility can get you meetings with influential people, as well as connections and interviews for potential future employment.

AFTER THE WIN

The first thing you must do after you win is find out the members of the committee, contact them, and sincerely thank all of them for awarding you the scholarship. If you interviewed with them personally, this step is especially important because it serves several purposes. First, you become cemented in their minds as a very grateful winner (which you are). Second, you obtain their contact information so you can remain in touch with them throughout your career. These are great people to have in your network for future opportunities involving both scholarships and jobs.

A hand-written note is more personal than an email and will encourage the committee members to remember you in the future.

Write each person a sincere, hand-written thank you note, and deliver it in person. A hand-written note is more personal than an email and will encourage the committee members to remember you in the future. Additionally, ask if you can obtain the address of the donor or the donor family so you may also send them a thank you. The donor will be impressed by the quality of students being selected for the award and will likely be willing to give more to the school or foundation. You could potentially be rewarded either in receiving an increased monetary award of that scholarship, or by being considered for other awards. Families with enough wealth to donate large sums of money to fund scholarships are great to have in your network and can assist you later when looking for an "in" at your dream job, so connect with them as early as possible.

THANK YOU GUIDELINES

The thank you letter should contain the following information:

1. *Describe what you will use the money for or how it will help you.*
2. *Explain why you chose to attend your particular university and what you enjoy most about it.*
3. *Highlight a few things you do around campus and your accomplishments as a student, as well as something you are passionate about.*
4. *Talk about your goals for the future and your path to achieving them.*
5. *Thank him or her again and offer your contact information.*

Following these five steps expresses your gratitude and puts you in a position to connect with these influential people further.

BUILD AND MAINTAIN RELATIONSHIPS

After being selected, remain in contact periodically with those who selected you, as well as your fellow winners. These are successful people, so it's a good idea to have them in your network. Surrounding yourself with a high level group of friends challenges you to push yourself even harder in order to achieve your goals. In doing so, you work effectively and intelligently because it requires a small amount of effort, yet has a big impact on your life.

Thank the people in your network that helped you win the scholarship as well. Winning is a result of the advice and assistance of many people. Thanking these people allows them to share the enjoyment of your accomplishment with you and also increases the likelihood of gaining their help in the future.

POSITIVE IMAGE

As a scholarship winner, you are in an elite group of students, especially if it is a big-name or selective scholarship. You represent the university both to the donors and to the other students, and at the same time, carry the confidence of the selection committee with you in your actions. Do not take this lightly. You must stay on the path that won you the scholarship in the first place, and you must continue working hard and staying involved. If the committee continually sees you as an outstanding student, your winnings will likely snowball, and you will be sought out for more and more scholarships and other great opportunities.

MAINTAIN ELIGIBILITY

Many of the scholarships you win will renew automatically, as long as you maintain the requirements. However, once you fall below the requirements, the schools tend to be very strict in their policies to revoke the automatic renewal feature. That's not to say you couldn't win it back by talking with the right people and regaining their confidence, but it is always best to keep yourself on track and well above the minimum requirements. You didn't win the scholarship by doing the minimum, and you shouldn't settle for less than your best after your win, so maintain your course of success.

RENEWAL REQUEST

Many larger scholarships automatically renew for either two or four years. However, if you find out yours isn't renewable, speak with those people on the committee you have remained in contact with to ask if there is any possibility of renewing it. Describe how the scholarship has allowed you to accomplish your goals, and present details on how you have contributed to the campus community because of it. The better the case you make for renewal, the better the chance you have for getting it renewed.

TURN A LOSS INTO FUTURE WINS

In the event you aren't selected for a scholarship, don't be discouraged. Take this opportunity to learn from your mistakes. Every loss puts you one step closer to success, if you choose to learn from it. So lose with class while making sure you learn a few key lessons. You have already been through the process of putting together an application, which will make future applications easier to prepare. And it's still important to get in touch with the committee, thank them for the opportunity, and ask them what you could do differently to improve your competitive position.

Even in a loss you show determination and the will to improve and try again. Each time you apply for a scholarship, you improve your skills more and more, so seek out as many as you can and you will eventually win some. Keep in mind that many scholarships are awarded to older students, so as you build your skills and reputation in the early years, you lay the foundation for acquiring money in the later years of your college career. No matter what, you must never give up and always keep improving yourself. Someone will notice and you will be rewarded.

> Keep in mind that many scholarships are awarded to older students, so as you build your skills and reputation in the early years, you lay the foundation for acquiring money in the later years of your college career.

FAST-TRACK YOUR CAREER

Not only will you graduate with little or no debt if you follow these steps and maximize your scholarship winnings, but also you will be on the fast track to great achievement. Without major loans you will be ahead of most college graduates, and therefore, you will be in a position of freedom to do what you are passionate about, not to mention have the ability to invest more money earlier to take advantage of the power of compound interest, as discussed in Chapter one.

In addition, if you followed these steps you have created a very solid network and you can leverage and use this network to your advantage. It's not what you know, but who you know, and the majority of job positions are filled based on preexisting relationships. When looking for a job, concentrate on your passions and put your network to work for you. Let your network know your interests, and ask for recommendations on what to do or who to talk with. Being a scholarship winner, you have the confidence of many people, and they will be willing to help you. All you need to do is ask and act on their recommendations.

key takeaways
from chapter 10

1   You must be a smart and gracious winner.

2   Write handwritten thank you notes to everyone involved.

3   Maintain the relationships you worked so hard to build.

4   Take time to understand the scholarship renewal guidelines.

5   A loss isn't the end of the world. Reuse the appropriate materials, and go for the next win.

final
thoughts
to consider

REDUCING THE COST OF YOUR EDUCATION VIA STRATEGIC PLANNING AND SCHOLARSHIPS IS GREAT, BUT YOU CAN RUIN ALL YOUR HARD WORK BY MAKING POOR SPENDING DECISIONS.

Whereas the worst financial decision is blindly acquiring student loans, the silliest financial decision is wasting scholarship money on an unaffordable rockstar lifestyle.

Hit reset. This is the best advice that exists when it comes to learning how to manage your lifestyle while in college. Forget everything you have grown to take for granted in regards to your family's lifestyle. Forget vacations, forget stocked fridges, forget dining out, forget the perfect sweater for the first day of class. You are officially broke now. But, who cares?

Why shouldn't you be broke? You are attempting to pay for something (a college education) with very few financial resources (because you are avoiding student loans). Math, your old friend from elementary school, tells you spending more money than you

have will lead to debt. Therefore, if you don't have much money, then your chances of dipping into debt greatly increase when your non-education expenses become a factor. This means you must live simply and smartly.

College is a wonderful social experience. But the level of wonderfulness is not dependent on how much money you spend. In fact, the same will be true for the rest of your life. The misconception that you need a large amount of money in order to have a good time is dangerous. We are talking about entertainment, here. Your entertainment spending should be based on your entertainment budget, not the other way around. Which brings us to a bigger point. You need a budget.

A budget can be as simple or as complicated as you want to make it, but a simple budget is still better than no budget at all. Don't be intimidated by the concept of budgeting. It primarily deals with addition and subtraction, and well, if you can't do that, then you probably shouldn't spend any money on college in the first place. Here are the basic steps to create a college student's budget.

1. A budget should be based on your income

Your income, in this instance, would be the income from the business you started, the job you have, or the scholarship checks you receive to pay for your college expenses. You cannot spend money you don't have, so make sure your expenses don't add up to more than your income. This seems like a very simple point, but if you understand it, you will be at a distinct advantage in relation to your peers.

2. Don't blow all your money on housing

In most cases, the living conditions you have during college are not as comfortable as the living conditions you have while living with your parents. That's okay. While you certainly don't want to live in a downtrodden, unsafe place, you do need to find a very modest living arrangement. The key here is roommates. Get roommates. The more incomes (as described above) used to pay for expenses, the cheaper expenses will get for you. This will allow you to pool your money with others and find reasonable housing.

3. Ditch the car, if you can

Convenience costs money. A car brings convenience. Thus, a
car costs money. College campuses are generally centralized
around a specific geographic area. Live in this area. Don't drive
home every weekend to see your parents. Don't drive out of
town for a weekend away. Just live a simple, cheap lifestyle. This
may be the only four years of your life that you can do it without
major side effects. From time to time you may need a car. Borrow one. Let someone else pay for the convenience of having a
car on campus. For adults in the workforce, 15% is generally an
acceptable percentage of income to spend on transportation.
For a college student? How about 0%?

4. Ramen is legendary for a reason

Have you heard of ramen? It's a very inexpensive noodle dish
that has been a staple on college campuses for decades. Students eat it because it's easy to prepare, relatively delicious, and
most importantly, cheap. This isn't to suggest that you only eat
ramen noodles. This is to suggest that your food budget should
reflect the qualities found in ramen noodles. A household of
four generally spends between $600-$1200 per month on food.
Your food budget in college can't come anywhere near these
numbers.

5. Peers can affect spending

Financial peer pressure is tough. If the people you spend a
majority of your time with make poor spending decisions, then
you will be more likely to make poor spending decisions. This
too will continue throughout your whole life. Get a grip on
your self-control now, and show confidence in your ability to go
through college on a budget.

ONE LAST WORD ON PARENTS

In Chapter two you learned that parent student loans were just as bad as student loans. While it's quite loving of your parents to put their financial future on the line in order to help you through college, it's completely unnecessary, and in fact, inappropriate.

You must cut the financial ties to your parents as soon as possible. The problem is, sometimes they don't make it easy. They love you and want to help you. Many parents think that helping you means bailing you out of tough financial situations. This is why it's hard. If you are in a tough financial position, your parents' assistance may seem like a life raft. It's not.

The longer you are financially dependent on your parents, the harder it will be to break this dependence. And this dependence can ruin your financial life. If you are still accepting financial assistance from your parents in your twenties, then you are only hurting yourself. You are forcing yourself to falsely afford your lifestyle. That is a no win situation. You must cut yourself off before your parents even bring it up. Cutting yourself off financially is the right thing to do. Your parents' successes are their own, not yours. You should not ride their financial coattails. If you want to leverage your parents' relationships and business associations in the professional world, use the skills that you learned in this book to do so. Just remember, the longer you drink from the money teat of your parents, the stronger the addiction becomes. Make a clean break.

AVOID STUDENT LOANS

You can accomplish your goal of graduating from college debt free. It takes a focused, sustained effort and a tremendous amount of planning, but compare that to the decade (or more) of financial ruin you will face with student loans. Initially, you need to look for ways to reduce the cost of your education altogether. This process starts in high school. If college funding continues to be an issue, then you need to consider starting a high-income earning business.

But as you learned, the ultimate tool for avoiding student loans is scholarships. Finding scholarships isn't enough, though. You need to win them. You need to form sincere, strategic relationships that will help you become a better student, and thus a better scholarship applicant. All of the processes you learned in this book are healthy. You learned what it means to be involved. You learned how to build and maintain relationships. But most importantly, you learned what strategic planning can accomplish.

These skills will serve you for the rest of your life. In fact, these skills, combined with zero student loan debt, will put you in elite company upon graduation from college. The bottom line is this: your career path and your financial life get easier when you choose to Avoid Student Loans.

Learn more about how to Avoid Student Loans, and sign up for the ASL Advanced Coaching Program at AvoidStudentLoans. com. For more information on making great financial decisions throughout your life, visit *PeteThePlanner.com.*

ABOUT THE AUTHORS

Peter Dunn (a.k.a. Pete the Planner), is responsible for some of the most cutting edge financial advice around. Whether he is preventing high income earners from wasting their opportunities or teaching single parents how to raise financially adjusted children, Pete the Planner always arrives to the scene with his trademark comedic wit.

He released his first book, *What Your Dad Never Taught You About Budgeting*, in 2006 and is the host of the popular radio show, *The Pete the Planner* show, on 93 WIBC FM. He was also the mastermind behind 24 Hour News 8's *60 Days to Change* and has appeared regularly on Fox News, Fox Business, CNN Headline News and numerous nationally syndicated radio programs.

His second book, *60 Days to Change: A Daily How To Guide With Actionable Tips to Improve Your Financial Life* was released in December of 2009.

In 2012, Peter was named one of the top four most influential personal finance experts in the nation by Cision Broadcasting. Peter was named one of "Indy's Best and Brightest" in finance in 2007 and media in 2009 by KPMG and was declared one of *NUVO* magazine 's "30 under 30 to Watch in the Arts" for comedy (back when he was young and funny). He won an Indiana Broadcasters Association Award in 2011 for the program he created, *500 Ways To Save*. Peter was awarded the Distinguished Young Alumni Award by Hanover College in 2012.

When not wrapped up in writing or dabbling in broadcast, Pete the Planner enjoys cooking and spending time with his wife, Sarah, and his daughter, Ollie.

Aaron Martin is a recent honors graduate of the Indiana University Kelley School of Business. He based his strategy in the book from his experience in being awarded several major scholarships.

He majored in finance and entrepreneurship and after college was selected as an Orr Fellow where he worked in the software industry. Currently he is the founder and CEO of AFM Enterprises, a fast-growing service company with hundreds of customers, and in a post-bachelor, pre-med program following his dream of becoming a doctor. He lives in Carmel, IN.

avoid student loans

AvoidStudentLoans.com

CPSIA information can be obtained
at www.ICGtesting.com
Printed in the USA
BVHW01s0227181217
503089BV00019B/1252/P

9 780983 458807